SUCCESSFUL
TELEPHONE
SELLING
IN THE '80s

SUCCESSFUL TELEPHONE SELLING IN THE '80s

Martin D. Shafiroff
and Robert L. Shook

▥ BARNES & NOBLE BOOKS
A DIVISION OF HARPER & ROW, PUBLISHERS
New York, Cambridge, Philadelphia
San Francisco, London, Mexico City
São Paulo, Sydney

SUCCESSFUL TELEPHONE SELLING IN THE '80S. Copyright © 1982 by Martin D. Shafiroff and Robert L. Shook. All rights reserved. Printed in the United States of America. No part of this book may be used or reproduced in any manner whatsoever without written permission except in the case of brief quotations embodied in critical articles and reviews. For information address Harper & Row, Publishers, Inc., 10 East 53rd Street, New York, N.Y. 10022. Published simultaneously in Canada by Fitzhenry & Whiteside Limited, Toronto.

First BARNES & NOBLE BOOKS edition published 1983.

ISBN: 0-06-463569-4 (previously ISBN: 0-06-014952-3)

88 89 90   10 9

To the memory of my mother
ETTA SHAFIROFF

M.D.S.

Acknowledgments

To Dick Ary, Lisa Avery, Diana Bloch, Bill Bresnan, Bob Burnett, Shelby Carter, Jr., Nancy Cone, Jeanne Desy, Shaindy Fenton, Bill Frankenstein, Joe Gandolfo, Joe Girard, Stan Glick, Janis Graber, Bettye Hardeman, Joanne Katz, Bob Knowlton, Irv Levey, Peter Nedostup, Rich Port, Greg Rice, John Rice, Buck Rodgers, Larry Schneider, Richard Schultz, Carrie Shook, Gary Siegrist, Paul Stang, Herbert Swartout, Barbara Tollis, Alan Weiler, and Nina Wood.

Contents

Preface

When my publisher asked me to write this book, I immediately began contacting leading telephone salespersons across the country to find out how they achieved their outstanding results. Among the people I called was Martin Shafiroff, a managing director with the prestigious investment banking firm Lehman Brothers Kuhn Loeb in New York City. In 1978 I had written a chapter on Marty in my book *Ten Greatest Salespersons,* * and I personally believed him to be America's number-one investment salesperson.

When I asked Marty to give me some ideas on how he generates hundreds of millions of dollars in securities transactions over the telephone, his response overwhelmed me. He had a conceptual understanding of telephone selling that far surpassed anything I had ever heard. Martin's desire to improve the quality of telephone selling and my persistence led to our working agreement on this book.

The prospect of co-writing a book with the man I believed to be the world's most effective salesperson on the telephone excited me. Minutes after the agreement I was on the telephone with Irv Levey at Harper & Row, who endorsed the idea enthusiastically.

When the Shafiroff-Shook writing team first embarked on this book, we worked for an entire weekend at facing desks. As we exchanged sales concepts and ideas for the use of the telephone in nearly every kind of business, we decided that writing was no exception. It would not only be convenient, it would be appropriate to work on our manuscript via long distance. So, for the following

*Harper & Row.

six months we collaborated between New York City and Columbus, Ohio—until the manuscript was completed. Never let it be said that the authors of this book don't practice what they preach!

As I collected material from Marty I became convinced that we were writing the best book ever written on telephone selling. Not only did we have our combined experience to draw on, but we were receiving support from hundreds of top salespersons throughout the country who were also eager to share their knowledge. This book is based not on theory but on proven field-tested techniques. To help you respond to various challenges on the telephone, we have detailed many actual selling experiences of my co-author as well as other top salespersons from across the United States. After you read about their experiences, you'll understand how much skill is involved in professional telephone selling.

While Marty uses the telephone to sell investments, the principles and techniques of telephone selling can be applied to many different industries. Regardless of your field, you will find that every technique given in this book can be applied, with minor adaptations, to your own sales strategy. So, learn from the very best how to sell your product or service over the telephone!

—ROBERT L. SHOOK

Introduction

Successful Telephone Selling in the '80s is not a theoretical book on what *ought* to work. The methods given here *do* work, for the most successful salespeople in the country. You can incorporate every single technique into your own selling; and *these techniques will increase your sales production.*

You may have tried telephone selling a few times and found that it didn't seem to work. But there would be no need for this book if all you had to do was pick up the telephone and sell. Successful selling over the telephone, as with personal sales visits, depends on learning the right techniques and practicing them. Once you do, telephone selling will work for you, because it can work for everyone!

Moreover, as this book will also demonstrate, almost *anything* can be sold on the telephone. Sure, everyone knows that in certain industries the telephone has been the conventional marketing tool for years; the selling of securities is a prime example. But products rarely associated with telephone selling can also be sold by phone —including high-ticket items like life insurance, real estate, and even fine art. One reason this is true is that today's businesspeople spend a major portion of their time on the telephone, often averaging three or four hours a day. Not only are they accustomed to doing business by phone, but they often prefer to, as a means of saving time. So whatever your product or service, don't think it can be sold only by a personal visit.

Only a few years ago, many sales managers viewed the telephone as the favorite escape of the lazy salesperson. Whatever he *said* he was accomplishing, the salesperson who was at his desk talking on the telephone during the day was a prime candidate for a lecture on how to use time productively.

In 1973, when the OPEC oil embargo touched off a dramatic increase in the cost of energy, all this began to change. American industry found that spiraling inflation was pushing the cost of sales visits up year after year. By 1980, the average cost of a personal sales visit to an industrial customer had passed the $100 mark! Suddenly, from a cost-benefit point of view, telephone selling made a lot of sense, and the phones went back on the desks. It was becoming clear that a sales force could generate a higher volume at a lower cost by incorporating the telephone into the overall strategy.

Today almost all salespersons use the telephone as a significant part of their daily routines, and good sales managers encourage them to do so. Even a quick look at the cost of air travel, gasoline, lodging, and meals reveals the economy of communicating by phone. The purpose of this book, however, is not to talk about reducing expenses but to focus on how to dramatically increase your sales production through using the telephone. Super salespersons have always known that the telephone is an invaluable asset; today the vast army of salespersons across the country are beginning to follow their lead.

The telephone also increases the size of your market. Virtually everyone in the United States can be reached by phone. And if an in-person call is necessary after a telephone appointment has been made, every major market in the country is less than a day away. A salesperson in Chicago or New York, for instance, is only a one-hour plane ride from more than 100 million people. Yes, in today's telemarketing world, distance must be measured in time, not miles.

As Americans, we are fortunate to have at our fingertips the world's finest telephone system. While it may have its flaws, our system far surpasses any other in the world. If you doubt this, ask somebody who has visited Russia how many hours it takes to place a long-distance call in that country. The ability to inexpensively sell and prospect by telephone, both locally and all over the country, is uniquely American.

However, success is not just a matter of picking up the receiver and launching forth. With telephone selling, as with anything else, there are right ways and wrong ways to do it. As you read this book, you will discover the methods that work for the top telephone salespersons in the country, methods that can guarantee your success, too. Please forget any preconceived notions you may have had about the limitations of telephone selling. Accept the idea that the telephone can be used to sell almost anything to anyone. Once you do, *Successful Telephone Selling in the '80s* will open new horizons for you—and give you the opportunity to maximize your potential.

SUCCESSFUL TELEPHONE SELLING IN THE '80s

The Telephone:
A Cost, Time,
and Energy Saver

Modern advances in computers, aerospace, and electronic technology have been astonishing. Yet the telephone, invented over a hundred years ago, still ranks as our number one technological sales tool. The reasons are evident. What businessperson doesn't place a high value on time? Who isn't concerned about spiraling costs and rising overhead? The telephone saves time, money, and energy.

SAVING MONEY

As recently as the 1960s, a gallon of gasoline sold for less than forty cents. For under ten dollars, a traveling salesperson could rent a decent motel room for the night. For another ten dollars, he could eat three good meals a day. Needless to say, these costs have skyrocketed. Whether you travel by automobile or airplane, getting there will cost you considerably more than it used to. Internal office expenses have risen correspondingly. In 1970 the average cost of a business letter dictated to a secretary was $3.05; by 1980 the price tag was $6.07.*

While other costs have risen steadily, the relative cost of telephone service has declined. For example, in 1949 the average industrial employee worked five hours and fifteen minutes to pay his monthly telephone bill. In 1979 the same industrial worker worked only one hour and twenty-two minutes for the same purpose. Fewer hours of work are now required to purchase most goods

*Dartnell Institute of Business Research, Chicago, Illinois.

and services, but even so, the cost of telephone service has risen much less, proportionately, than the cost of the average commodity. Between 1973 and 1979, for instance, consumer prices in general rose nearly 70 percent, but the cost of residential telephone service went up only 14 percent.* Telephone service is cheaper now, both in real terms and relative to the rest of the economy, than at any time in history.

Every business today has had to intensify its concern about expenses. In the past, sales volume alone was often considered the best indicator of success. However, in recent years numerous companies have experienced record revenues only to find them offset by record losses. The question must always be asked: What are the costs of attaining higher sales volume? Before any decision about sales strategy is made, the cost of the strategy involved must be determined.

Sometimes a company will be on the brink of disaster before it is willing to revise its sales methods. A small Iowa-based company, for instance, lost four of its five sales representatives before it turned to telephone selling. One by one, the salespersons had resigned, complaining that at least one-third of the accounts they called on were no longer in the market for heating or air-conditioning supplies, or had gone out of business altogether. The salespersons weren't making any money—and neither was the company.

In desperation, the manager and the remaining salesman laid out a telephone strategy. So the account files could be straightened out, the first stage called for the salesman to simply "qualify" customers by phone—that is, to make sure they had both the need and the ability to pay for the company's products. When this resulted in a number of orders being placed, the sales strategy was rapidly revised. Now, all selling is done by this one salesman—who produces more orders than all five did on the road! In analyzing results, the company realized that each personal sales visit to a local or out-of-town client, *whether it was productive or not,* had cost about

*"Relative Cost of Telephone Service 1940–1979," American Telephone and Telegraph Company, Economic Analysis Section, November 1979.

twenty dollars. The telephone "sales visits" had cost the company approximately one-tenth as much.

SAVING TIME

In analyzing sales methods, the cost in time is of prime importance. Time *is* money; the failure to recognize that can be fatal. Every salesperson must determine how to get the highest possible return on the time and energy he invests. Experienced salespersons know that their time is their most valuable asset—and guard it jealously. But the majority of salespeople actually spend a relatively small portion of their total working hours productively. It has been estimated that in the fields of real estate, insurance, and securities, the average sales representative wastes as much as 80 percent of his selling time.

A salesperson making outside visits in person runs into a long list of problems which consume time during the course of the day, most of the problems unavoidable. For example, there are traffic tie-ups, automobile breakdowns, poor driving conditions, long waits in reception areas, and broken appointments. Needless to say, the telephone salesperson does not have to cope with any of these time-wasters.

If, by proper use of the telephone, a salesperson can increase the percentage of time he spends presenting his product or service, his production will also increase. In other words, if two salespersons have roughly equal ability, the one who gives twice as many presentations will produce at least twice as many sales. When, through careful time management, a salesperson increases his selling time three-, four-, or fivefold, his production should increase by at least the same amount. Moreover, the principle of synergy applies: it is possible to have a far greater return in additional production than the actual increase in sales presentations. Twice as many presentations may result in three or four times as many sales.

In discussing the performance of salespersons who doubled the number of presentations they made every day, sales managers verify that their sales volume usually more than doubled. It seems likely that these salespersons became more skilled at giving their presentations, and more adept at overcoming objections, simply because they got so much more experience.

The most conscientious and disciplined salesperson may inadvertently waste time in face-to-face sales, as one large lumber company found out. In order to analyze the profitability of its sales program, the company began by observing a number of salespeople during a typical day—always a good approach. They found that an outside salesperson normally visited eight customers a day. On the average, two of these daily visits did not result in talking with a buyer. They were wasted.

When the company applied these figures to its entire sales force, it found that of about 60,000 visits to customers each year, 15,000 were wasted! That represented almost 2,000 sales days and 150,000 miles of travel that were totally unproductive. Even more shocking was the estimate that this wasted time—over five years of selling time—meant that $4 million a year in sales were not being made.

A company cannot ignore figures like that. While this company had no intention of bringing its outside salespeople into the office, the managers did institute a two-pronged program. First, salespeople must telephone for appointments instead of just dropping by. Second, salespeople must set up a system for contacting customers by telephone between visits to inform them of price changes, promotions, and new products. As a result of these policies, numerous orders are placed without a personal visit at all, and it is unusual for a salesperson to make a wasted call. Because the sales representatives have appointments, wasted driving time and downtime spent in reception areas has been significantly reduced.

Shelby Carter, Jr., senior vice president of marketing at Xerox, calls downtime "windshield time." "You don't raise sales productivity," Shelby states, "with sales representatives driving as fast as possible over the countryside to get in a few extra calls." Xerox, like many other companies, has found the telephone indispensable in reducing the "windshield time" of its sales representatives.

INSTANT RESPONSE

Businesses often use letters to handle details that could be taken care of by telephone. The high cost of a business letter has already been mentioned, but another factor must also be taken into account: a telephone generates instant response.

In any form of communication, misunderstanding is possible; but it is less likely during a telephone conversation. Why? Because the person at the other end of the line can react immediately. If he doesn't understand something, he can ask a question. If he has an objection, he can make it, and *you* have an opportunity to respond. Misunderstandings, requests for information, and objections that could take weeks to clear up by mail can be handled in a few moments in conversation.

Essential to good communication is the verification process. In conversation, the salesperson can verify that the client understands what he is saying—and he can verify it instantly. The margin for error is greatly reduced, and that can mean much time and money saved for both parties.

EXPANDING YOUR TERRITORY

Because the telephone saves time and spans distance, a salesperson who uses it is virtually unrestricted by geography. A stockbroker, for instance, can become registered in all states; when he does, his territory is coast-to-coast. While a broker may restrict himself to one city, or even one area of the city, and use the telephone effectively in this territory, he may also choose to "go national." If he does, a customer who lives three thousand miles away is as close as his phone. "My market is anywhere and everyone," says one broker. Regardless of what you sell, the telephone offers you the choice of expanding your territory. If you are restricted from doing this either by government regulations or by company policy, at the very least you can use the telephone to cover your territory more effectively.

Joe Gandolfo, who is considered the world's leading life insurance agent, sells several hundred million dollars' worth of life insurance a year. With the sizable policies Joe specializes in, he did not want to be limited to working a small territory around his home in Lakeland, Florida. Licensed to sell life insurance throughout the United States, Joe calls prospects long distance to set up appointments.

"It would be impossible for me to travel the way I do," he says, "and not be a heavy user of the telephone." Joe estimates that by using long-distance to set up appointments he reduces his expenses by more than $100,000 a year. And that figure represents only overhead; the value of the time he saves is far more.

Obviously, it would be foolhardy for any salesperson who calls on clients in faraway locations to work without confirmed appointments. What person in his right mind would want to fly from New York to Los Angeles without having specific appointments scheduled in advance? In some cases, a week's trip may involve as many as a hundred telephone calls to set up twenty-five sales presentations in advance, but the overall time savings will still be significant. With the use of the telephone, many salespersons can save enough time to expand their territories, sometimes from coast to coast.

SERVICING MARGINAL ACCOUNTS

While every account is valuable, the businessperson must always consider the cost of doing business with a customer. The cost of a personal sales visit to an industrial customer rose from $42.92 in 1967* to well over $100 in 1980, an increase of more than 235 percent. While major accounts may continue to justify personal service calls, other accounts must be classified as "marginal." If they are to be maintained at all, they must be serviced less expensively. For such accounts, servicing by telephone may be the best solution.

Most companies have a number of accounts which may or may

*Laboratory of Advertising Performance Report #8013.4, McGraw-Hill Research.

not pay for themselves. All too often, the sales manager imposes a blanket policy: "We've always gone for eyeball-to-eyeball contact with our customers. In this industry, that's the way it's done." But whatever has been done in the past, the skyrocketing cost of fuel, coupled with spiraling inflation, means that nobody can afford to ignore the actual cost of the sales visit, especially to an account which is only marginally profitable.

An objection often made to telephone selling is that the telephone call will not generate the same volume of business as the personal visit. While this may be true, doing business via the telephone may nevertheless be more profitable. Consider the relative costs. While the industrial sales visit costs over $100, McGraw-Hill Research* reveals that the telephone sales call averages $3.50. With these costs in mind, an individual businessperson can evaluate marginal accounts. Can the company afford $100 for an on-the-spot service call to company X? If not, can the customer's needs be satisfied by partial telephone servicing of the account?

Cosway Pharmaceuticals has a typical problem servicing accounts. The company's representative, Joe Cunningham, services Michigan, with a large number of accounts in the Detroit area. In the Upper Peninsula, several hundred miles north of Detroit, Joe also has nine accounts in nine different small towns. While each account generates only minor sales volume, a one-day trip to service them periodically could probably be justified. But Joe has another problem—the buying cycle. Usually, no two accounts are ready to place an order at the same time. If he does visit all nine small-town accounts, he will find that while one customer needs to restock, another wants to wait three weeks. Still a third says, "Come back in December," and a fourth says, "I'll give you an order in February."

If these accounts shared the same buying cycle, it would be marginally profitable to service them in person. But we don't all run out of shampoo and toothpaste at the exact same time, and neither

*McGraw-Hill Research, August 1977, McGraw-Hill Publications Co., New York, N.Y.

do all Joe's customers run out of Cosway products at the same time. So it is impossible to service them all on one trip. For this group of accounts, telephone servicing is the only sensible answer.

MAKING APPOINTMENTS

Making a solid appointment by telephone for an in-person sales presentation is a great time-saver, even if a salesperson services a local territory. For one thing, every salesperson has had the experience of waiting in a company reception area, perhaps for an hour or more, only to discover that he has been waiting for the wrong person! According to the McGraw-Hill study, "65 percent of all sales calls are made on the wrong person." Over a period of a year, such misunderstandings can result in weeks or months of wasted time. Doesn't it make more sense to call ahead and make an appointment—with the right prospect?

Along the same line, a salesperson may be given leads, perhaps as a result of inquiries, which turn out to be fruitless. By calling these leads to make an appointment, the salesperson can find out whether the prospect is still interested. If not, a wasted trip is saved.

Even salespersons who believe their products must always be sold face to face often use the telephone to set up appointments with qualified prospects. For these salespersons, making appointments by phone eliminates unnecessary travel and reduces both waiting time and calls on unqualified prospects.

Certain industries whose products are almost never sold by telephone nevertheless depend on the telephone for setting up appointments. A real estate agent, for instance, wouldn't try to sell a home that had not been seen by the prospect. But the same agent might use the telephone to screen potential buyers and make appointments to gain listings. In addition to screening out prospects who are definitely not interested, the telephone interview may be a means to whet the prospect's appetite to the point where he grants an in-person interview.

Successful appointment making depends on the salesperson's

ability to create initial interest, so that the prospect wants to learn firsthand about the product or service offered. In effect, the selling process has two stages. First, a call must be made to get the appointment. Then, when that has been achieved, the salesperson can sell his product or service.

Often when a sales interview is scheduled by telephone, a salesperson's self-confidence is bolstered. Shelby Carter explains that now "the sales representative is better prepared for the call. He feels more professional in performing his job, and has a higher order rate per call. He walks into the customer's office with confidence, knowing that the customer is expecting him." This added confidence is an important bonus of scheduling appointments by telephone.

Making appointments can dramatically increase a salesperson's effectiveness. A North Carolina furniture manufacturer had advertised a new line of grandfather clocks, suitable for display in gift boutiques and craft stores as well as furniture and department stores. The advertisements attracted a large number of inquiries from prospective retailers. But the sales representatives handling the line over a large territory were able to call on only three or four prospects a day. Only one in twenty of their calls actually led to an order. After three months the company had lost so much money that it considered dropping the line.

Instead, the sales reps were trained to use the telephone to follow up the inquiries and to make appointments with the prospects. One day of the week was set aside for this purpose. Through these calls, the salespersons were able to weed out the dead inquiries and to make sure that they would be calling on interested prospects. Because their calls were by appointment, waiting was reduced. Inquiries were handled more swiftly, and the closing ratio increased from one order out of twenty calls to one out of three. The grandfather clock became one of the strongest lines in the company's seventy-eight-year history.

CONSERVING ENERGY

A company may also have broader reasons for changing its sales strategy. In 1974, when Xerox Corporation began searching for ways to use the telephone in selling, it had both internal and external concerns. "Windshield time" was a problem, but management was also searching for ways to lessen fuel consumption. Among the new programs instituted was the use of the telephone by sales representatives to make appointments.

In the past, Xerox representatives had made cold calls, and many company managers were not in favor of the change. But it soon became evident that calling for appointments was just as effective as the old way. In terms of the savings in time and money, the company has been well satisfied with the new policies.

Shelby Carter also comments on the broader concern. "Intelligent energy conservation measures, such as gasohol, more fuel-efficient cars, and synthetic fuel are being developed," he notes. "We can also affect this nation's consumption of oil and natural resources through a more intelligent use of the telephone. And the telephone is not a concept, it's a reality. It pays off today."

CONCLUSION

Unless your business is one in which customers come to you, and you have more business than you want, the chances are that a certain percentage of your selling should be on the telephone. Not only will it save money and conserve energy, but telephone selling is a highly productive use of your most valuable commodity—your time.

2

Using Your Time Profitably on the Telephone

Your time is your most valuable asset. Study any successful salesperson and you will observe an individual who guards his time carefully. The outside salesperson described in Chapter 1 isn't alone in suffering from "windshield time." A telephone salesperson can also encounter endless distractions which divert his efforts and result in downtime. There's a great temptation for him to use his time for chores that aren't nearly as productive as his actual selling on the telephone. Making effective telephone calls must be his number one priority. Always remember, nothing happens until something is sold. And you can't produce sales without making contacts. This fact is so obvious that nothing else need be said about it. You've got a job to do, and it can be accomplished only when you're selling!

SETTING GOALS

The best assurance that you *will* concentrate on this number one priority is to have a daily goal. Every salesperson has two ways to get orders: he can service old accounts, and he can generate new accounts. Servicing old accounts is the subject of Chapter 9; first, let's concentrate on how setting daily goals can help a salesperson use his time to generate new accounts day after day, month after month.

The first mistake many people make when they begin telephone selling is to think in terms of the number of their calls. But the number of telephone calls made in a day is not important. If a salesperson makes fifty calls or one hundred calls and nothing results from them, he hasn't accomplished anything. His time is wasted. *The salesperson's first goal should be completions.*

A "completion" is a telephone call that actually gets through to the right individual. A call that is to be returned, or a discussion with an assistant or a secretary does not count. In this initial call, you briefly explain what you have in the way of a product or philosophy. You bring to the individual's attention what you have to offer, and you discover his interests. In some cases you will want to make an appointment for a face-to-face presentation; in other cases you will follow up with a letter or a later telephone call. But the completion is not aimed at getting an order. It is aimed only at finding out whether or not you can proceed with future contacts with this individual. He may say yes, he may say no. It's still a completion.

A realistic goal for a stockbroker is fifteen completions a day. All prime selling time is devoted to achieving that goal. When, at the end of the day, he has actually recorded fifteen completions, that is a major achievement. Experience suggests that this goal is reasonable for salespersons in many fields of products and services. But whatever number of completions is set as a goal, disciplining yourself to work toward that goal is an absolute prerequisite of success.

Once you have set a goal, the value of your time will become more evident. To get through to fifteen people, tell them what you have to offer, and discover whether they have any interest, you may have to make a hundred calls, spend time on hold, and call some individuals more than once. Obviously, it becomes necessary to hold down the amount of time spent on any individual phone call. You must set a time limit on each conversation with a prospect. There's a point of diminishing returns when your time spent with a client is no longer productive, and you must end the conversation and go on to your next call. Don't be shy about saying, "Mr. Jones, it's been a pleasure chatting with you this morning, but I am running late for an important meeting. Again I thank you for your business. Have a good day." He's probably busy too, and he'll respect you for placing a high value on both his and *your* time.

The number of yeses gained in fifteen completions will vary from one salesperson to another; for example, on the average a stockbroker should find that one out of three completions will be a yes: a person interested in further communication about this service. These yeses are now prospects. On a daily basis, you should be generating five prospects; that is twenty-five a week; one hundred a month; twelve hundred a year.

While a significant part of each day is devoted to making completions, no salesperson has to be told the importance of following up on good prospects. Much of this book will be devoted to turning prospects into clients through telephone presentations. It should be noted that an effective salesperson will convert about 25 percent of his prospects into accounts.

If you have twelve hundred completions a year, and do convert 25 percent into accounts, at the end of that year you will be richer by three hundred new accounts—a substantial achievement. A salesperson who can do that year after year is destined for success. But bear in mind that this kind of success comes down to setting and meeting the daily goal—fifteen, or however many, completions every day. As Benjamin Disraeli said, "The secret to success is constancy of purpose." Very good advice for telephone selling!

KEEPING RECORDS

You must record your progress on a daily basis. First, note the number of initial calls made. Second, keep a list of completions, the people you actually spoke to regarding your services. Third, record prospects, the group willing and interested in hearing from you. Fourth, note the daily number of presentations, the actual requests for orders, made to prospects. Fifth, keep a daily list of new accounts, the key to your growth.

Records like this have many advantages. First and most important, they give you a track to follow. You will have direction. Instead of wandering aimlessly through the day, you will know exactly where you stand in relation to your goals. Second, accurate record keeping helps you determine your shortcomings. If you attempt to call a hundred individuals and get through to only ten, you need to work on the techniques of getting past the people who screen calls. If, on the other hand, you do get through to thirty, and if 50 percent of them become prospects, you can congratulate yourself on your strong initial presentation.

The unfortunate truth is that most people do not follow an organized procedure, even one as simple as this. As a result, they have no idea how much time they waste during the course of a day. Anyone who has spent some time in sales has known salespeople who really believe they always put in a good day's work, but the bottom line was that most of their effort was misdirected, and they actually accomplished very little. Only when you put your goals and accomplishments down on paper can you really evaluate whether your time is spent productively. Remember that salespersons get paid for results—not just putting in time. *Productive time* is what counts!

As he qualifies an individual, a salesperson also needs a procedure for keeping notes on anything important he learns. Small file cards are often used as a convenient way to carry and store information. In the qualifying process, you have the opportunity to learn a great deal about the prospect, but this information could be forgotten unless it is recorded. The file card is your data bank, and it can be one of your most valuable assets as a salesperson.

During and after your initial conversation with the prospect, jot down notes on an index card. A stockbroker, for example, will record whatever the prospect has revealed about himself and his family; his financial goals; the kind of investment he is interested in; his prior investment experiences; and the dollar amount he usually commits to an order.

Every prospect should also be qualified with a number that represents an emotional rating and a factual one. The emotional rating relates to the feeling gained from the conversation. Did you have a good rapport with him? Will he welcome another call? Was he enthusiastic about your philosophy? Did he ask questions and become involved in the conversation? The factual rating reflects the prospect's ability to make a transaction, as far as you can determine this.

The prospect can be rated on a scale from one to five, with one being the highest. So if he has said, "That's great. I really need someone to work with me on my investments. I like your approach and I have a large amount of funds presently available for your suggestions," then he's rated a number one. He's excited about your concepts, and he has the financial resources to act now.

A five is the lowest rating acceptable for continued communication. It indicates that the prospect said yes reluctantly, sounded difficult, and indicated his financial resources were uncertain.

Accurate record keeping is especially important when a new account is opened. Immediately following your conversation with a new account, make a note on his 3 × 5 card of your impression of him and the conversation, and record all information concerning the transaction: for example, "5,000 shares of Great American Oil at 22." If he was excited about the investment, jot that down. Perhaps he told you that within the next few weeks he will have some cash coming in, and might be able to increase his position at that time. Note that.

Then, and this is a very significant function of records, make a note of the date you should call him next. Place the card in a chronological follow-up file, so that you make the call at the appropriate time. This is the kind of detail work that must be done in any field.

The value of keeping good records and analyzing them carefully is shown in the experience of a New York City shoe manufacturer. The firm had several sales representatives serving some 4,000 retail outlets in the eastern portion of the United States. In analyzing revenues, the vice president of marketing realized that the outside sales reps were understandably concentrating on the high-volume accounts. The smaller accounts were simply not being serviced adequately, and furthermore, the sales force was too busy to seek out new accounts. A natural result was that potentially good business was being overlooked.

The solution was to bring the sales representatives into the home office and set up a card file system. In a major effort, the selling cycle of every account, large and small, was analyzed, and a schedule was set up to call each account at the appropriate time. Four incoming and outgoing WATS lines were installed for this purpose. The company also sent full-color sales catalogs to each of its existing and potential accounts. The catalogs were loose-leaf with step-by-step instructions on how to insert replacement pages containing such information as new models available, discontinued models, price increases, etc. The sales reps then called every buyer to explain how to buy and reorder by using the catalogs and the incoming WATS lines.

After follow-up calls were made according to each account's buying cycle, the company began to realize substantial increases in its sales volume. Not only did the larger accounts place bigger orders, but the marginal ones increased too. Furthermore, the company opened up many new accounts which eventually became major customers. Within a year, there was a 250 percent increase in business.

USING PRIME TIME

Prime time includes those hours during the day (or evening) when a salesperson can reasonably be expected to make calls. The successful salesperson uses that time primarily for selling.

It is important to note that this definition is qualified by the words "can reasonably be expected to make calls." In some industries, the established working hours of nine to five are the only times a salesperson can reach a prospect. In other cases, a personal relationship with a client is a decisive factor. While an advertising executive might not feel comfortable calling one client after five, he could freely call another at home because they are golfing buddies. In most cases, common sense and discretion dictate when you can sell.

The salesperson whose territory is the entire United States has to schedule his calls with time zones in mind. While many people on the East Coast can be expected to be out to lunch at noon, the time is only nine o'clock on the West Coast, ten o'clock in the Mountain States, and eleven o'clock in the Midwest. If you're on the East Coast, you can thus make calls until eight P.M. and still not contact anybody after normal working hours. Likewise, many successful salespersons who live on the West Coast and serve a national territory start their selling day at six in the morning.

Your records should indicate vital information about a prospect's individual schedule. You might learn that a particular executive arrives at his office at seven-thirty in the morning—a good time to reach him and talk without interruption. Or a secretary may tell you that Mr. Jones is such a busy man that he works until seven at night—another clue. From prior experience you may know who takes an early lunch hour and is back in the office by twelve-thirty.

In short, for a salesperson simply to pick up the telephone and call people at random is doing it the hard way. A successful salesperson has a game plan, and his calls are already scheduled before prime time starts. Whether he has to be in the office an hour earlier or hire an assistant to do his scheduling is not the issue. The issue is, *homework is done in advance—not during prime time.* When you start your day, your list of calls should be on your desk; you should not lose an hour or more of selling time getting organized.

A very effective way to free up prime time is to hire an assistant. The assistant can help not only by scheduling but by getting the prospect or client on the line. This increases your contact pace and allows you to reach and influence more people.

The successful salesperson does not give in to the temptation to long lunches with his buddies. He does not read *The Wall Street Journal* or an industry newspaper during prime selling time. During those hours when he can transact business, he disciplines himself not to allow anything to interfere. His first priority during prime time is communicating with his clients.

SELF-DISCIPLINE

Coffee breaks, bull sessions around the water cooler, personal phone calls, and countless other distractions must not be allowed to cut into selling time. The important thing to remember is to *sell during prime selling time.* Every other function of your job should be performed during non-selling hours. Naturally, this is the ideal. A small portion of your day will inevitably be devoted to the unforeseen distractions and interruptions—the emergency, the unexpected problem—that throw you off the track. Everybody is subjected to this. But while the weak salesperson will spend most of his time responding to interruptions, the disciplined producer will not be sidetracked. He has a game plan, and he will not deviate from it. Rich Port, a successful Chicago Realtor and past president of the National Association of Realtors, says, "A successful salesperson disciplines himself or herself to make all the telephone calls he or she knows must be made every day." Along with many others, Rich is convinced that once a salesperson has committed himself to doing what has to be done, he will succeed.

Just as many salespersons believe they are being productive when they do busywork during prime selling time, many tend to neglect the necessary backup work. In each case, self-discipline is needed to *do what you are supposed to do.* There *is* essential paperwork, and there *are* mundane details in every job which cannot be neglected. Doing paperwork and making a schedule for your calls during the evening or early in the morning before the calls will require a higher level of energy, and it will mean working a longer day. But who ever said that doers don't pay a price for their success? If you observe the successful salespersons you know, you'll discover that they are people who possess good work habits. They value their selling time, and they are willing to find other time for routine details.

The discipline to set your goal, and to work toward it every day, using prime selling time only to sell, is essential to a top telephone salesperson.

CONCLUSION

Time is your most important asset. It is too frequently wasted on non-productive activities. In order to use your time effectively, you must set up priorities. Your goals must be adhered to on a daily basis, and written verification of your progress should be kept. The successful salesperson uses his prime time to sell. He doesn't allow himself to be sidetracked by non-essential work. His self-discipline is readily observed, and perhaps it is this quality, above all, that enables him to outproduce other would-be super salespersons. In short, effective time management and success are inseparable. The successful telephone salesperson is an individual who places a high value on his time—and uses it accordingly.

3.

Getting Through to the Right Person

Getting through to the right person is essential, whether you're selling over the telephone or face to face. Not only is a presentation to the wrong person a waste of time, but it can also jeopardize the sale. You may end up in a situation where the individual does not have the authority to say yes, but can say no! Now, that's a real no-win situation!

FINDING THE DECISION-MAKER

When you are dealing with a small sole-proprietor business, it usually isn't difficult to identify the individual with authority to make a decision; however, it isn't so cut and dried when calling a large organization for the first time. Naturally, when a reliable source has recommended a specific individual as the decision-maker, there isn't any problem. But without the advantage of such information, getting through to the right person may require some fairly fancy footwork on your part.

One individual who has developed a highly successful telephone technique for determining who has the authority to make a buying decision is Richard Schultz, the founder and chairman of National Revenue Corporation, the largest cash-flow management services firm in the world. "Your most valuable source of information," Richard says, "is the switchboard operator. Unlike a secretary, she is not there to screen; she's there to help. Let's say I want to contact General Express, a giant corporation. I don't simply call and ask to speak to the comptroller. Maybe they don't have a comptroller.

Or maybe he's not the one who makes the decision. Instead, I ask the switchboard operator, 'Who's in charge of Accounts Receivable?'

" 'Mr. Taft is. He's the manager of Accounts Receivable.'

" 'Who does he report to?'

" 'He reports to Mr. Berry, our comptroller.'

" 'May I ask who the comptroller reports to?'

" 'That's Mr. Brown.'

" 'And what's Mr. Brown's position?'

" 'He's the treasurer.'

" 'And who does he report to?'

" 'He reports to Mr. Gould. He's our vice president of finance.'

" 'And who does he report to?'

" 'He reports to our president.'

" 'Would you connect me with Mr. Gould, please.'

"Now I'm talking to the man who reports to the president. If it had been a smaller company (a small bank, for instance), I would try to talk directly with the president. I would always rather start at the top. If he's not the right person, he'll refer you to the right person. Then you are in the excellent position of being able to say, 'Jack Gould and I were talking, and he suggested I talk to you.' In other words, the boss sent me. But by using this technique, I guarantee you, within five minutes I can find the decision-maker for our services, I don't care how big the company is. Most salespersons don't talk to the right people, and that's why they end up telling their sales managers that they've got a dozen deals up in the air, but nothing is being sold!"

The second part of qualifying the decision-maker occurs when Richard actually calls the individual. After it has been established that the company has a problem, and that the prospect is willing to see him, he again qualifies with the question "Are you in a position to make a decision about a change for improvement in business policy today?" Even when the prospect says yes, Richard asks if there is somebody else, a partner perhaps, who should be present. He cautions, "He might say he's the decision-maker just to impress me with his importance. I want to make it easy for him to get somebody else there if that's necessary. I'll say, 'Can you think of anybody else that should be in on it?' This is one thing I'm not bashful about. You've got to talk to the decision-maker!"

Richard points out that often these are joint decisions. "If *he* can't make a decision," he adds, "I want to work real hard to have him admit it now, so I can talk to the decision-maker. And two people are always easier to sell than one. Three are easier than two; a whole group is easiest. Nobody likes to make a decision. With more than one, they share the responsibility, and they also look to the salesperson to help them make the decision."

While National Revenue's salespersons set up presentations for groups of people who share in the decision-making process, other salespersons often schedule a telephone conference call with the decision-makers. These conference calls are often the only way to get together a group of busy executives based in different parts of the country. Such a gathering in a single room would otherwise be very difficult and sometimes even impossible to arrange.

GETTING THROUGH THE THIRD PARTY, THE SCREENER

In most cases, a third party stands between the salesperson and the individual he is trying to reach. It may be a receptionist, an assistant, or a spouse. The most commonly encountered third party is probably the private secretary, and she is also the most skilled at screening calls. For that reason, our discussion will focus on the private secretary. However, no matter who the third party is, the same techniques apply.

In order to be successful, you must understand that the secretary's job is to screen calls and thereby save her boss's time. She must be convinced that he will want to talk to you, so she is the first person you have to influence. If you are not successful in doing that, you won't get a chance to approach the prospect—because you won't get through.

Your first approach should be brief and direct: "My name is John Smith, with United Corporation. May I please speak to Mr. Jones." There's no point in giving a long explanation of who you are or why you want to speak with him; the secretary is not the decision-maker. So identify yourself and ask to speak with the prospect. Frequently this is enough to put you through immediately.

You should present yourself in a pleasant and authoritative manner. Speak firmly. Do not hesitate; get right to the point! This approach influences the secretary's reaction. At this point she may tell her employer, "There's a Mr. Smith on the phone. He's with United Corporation and it sounds important. Shall I put him through?"

On the other hand, if she has reacted negatively, she will say, "There's someone on the phone from United Corporation. Just a salesman, I think. Shall I tell him you're busy?" Often the executive relies on her judgment. If she has this reaction, he will probably say, "Yes, tell him I'm busy and not interested." As you can see, the impression you make on that secretary is very important.

When you're calling successful executives, very often the secretary will attempt to get more information before she relays a message. After you identify yourself, she will usually ask, "Does he know you?" If he doesn't, and your call is not business-related, your reply should be "We haven't met, but I'm sure Mr. Jones is familiar with my company. The call does not relate to company matters. It's more personal than that." This response gives the secretary the basic information, creates a degree of curiosity, and frequently results in your getting through to the prospect.

Some intermediaries are super screeners. They want to know everything. They hold the power to deny you access to the prospect, and they enjoy that authority. It's very important that you recognize their influence and develop your selling skills to effectively handle the resistance they give you. Remember that they are only doing their jobs. An executive can't talk to every salesperson who calls, and it's up to the secretary to determine who's important enough to warrant his time. It's *your* job to make sure that she thinks you are important and promptly puts through your call.

It's possible that the secretary will at some point say, "Mr. Smith, if you're selling stocks [or whatever you sell], I know Mr.

Jones is not interested in talking to you. He asked me to tell any stockbrokers who call that he is satisfied with his present contacts."

At every point in your discussion with this third party, you must remember that your objective is not to leave the decision up to her. You must talk to the prospect. When she tries to make the decision for the prospect in this manner, your response depends on how you think about yourself. If you feel that your job is selling stocks, or real estate, or insurance, then you will say, "Fine. I won't call Mr. Jones anymore." It's really a matter of personal attitude. Are you just another salesperson, or do you have something unique to offer? Have you done your homework well and do you believe in your product? Do you believe in yourself and the benefits of what you offer? If so, don't categorize yourself as "just another salesperson."

In a pleasant and affirmative manner, say, "I want to emphasize that presently I have nothing specifically in mind for Mr. Jones. My call is more in the manner of a personal introduction. Mr. Jones will be familiar with United Corporation, and we would appreciate a few moments of his time."

Once you have said this, you have said it all. Now remain silent. The responsibility has shifted to her. She's been given enough justification to put you through, and that's the end of the conversation. It is an error to go any further in your explanation.

SPEAKING WITH AUTHORITY

Many examples in this book emphasize the importance of projecting confidence and authority. This is especially important in getting through the screener, whose job is to separate trivial calls from important ones. Bear in mind that she is not paid to keep *everyone* from talking to her boss—just to screen out the unimportant calls. Getting through the screener will never be a problem for you if you remember that *you are important.*

People you talk to on the telephone are instantly aware of your self-image, although they may not be conscious of it, and they respond accordingly. Therefore an air of authority is vital in dealing with the person who screens the prospect's calls. If you sincerely believe you have something important and unique to offer, the screener will believe it too, and will assist you in getting through. But you must believe it first. Only through your personal conviction can you generate the necessary authority. This is where getting through to the subject really begins—in your own mind.

National Revenue representatives are trained to maintain authority during the initial conversation with "the gatekeeper." Richard Schultz says, "Don't attempt to charm her. You must be very businesslike and official. A lot of salespersons try to 'win her over,' but she's onto their techniques. If you do that, she'll only become more suspicious that you're selling something, and then *she'll* control the interface between the two of you."

Richard also advises that a salesperson shouldn't sit for long periods of time "on hold." Important people value their time; if you let your time be wasted, you lose importance in her eyes. If the decision-maker is busy, get back to him. Demonstrate that your time is valuable, too.

In getting through the gatekeeper, many salespeople lose control by volunteering too much information. "Never tell her more than she asks," Richard stresses. "Give the briefest possible answer, and then ask *her* a question."

Although we have suggested giving your name and company name immediately, Richard prefers not to. Instead, he begins like this: " 'I'd like to talk to Mr. Johnson, please.' "

" 'May I tell him who's calling?'

" 'Richard Schultz. Is he in, please?'

" 'Yes, he is. What company are you with, Mr. Schultz?'

"Now," Richard says, "I speak very slowly. 'National Revenue. Would you tell him I'm on the phone, please?'

"At this point, I have asked her three times to connect me with him. Persistency pays off. This is a game of verbal volleyball. No matter how much you tell her, she'll come back with two or three screening questions—she feels that's her job. Therefore, when she asks who's calling, I don't say 'Richard Schultz of National Revenue.' I make her ask for the information. And I always answer her question with a question.

"If she's really persistent and asks the nature of my business, as a last resort I'll reply, 'It's a confidential financial matter. Would you please tell him that I would like to speak to him? If he's too busy, I'll be happy to call back.'

"What's the worst thing that can happen? When I finally do get to talk to him, he can say, 'Why didn't you tell her this was about collecting delinquent accounts?' My answer to that is 'At National Revenue, we believe that the collecting of delinquent accounts receivable is a confidential matter, and customers usually appreciate any efforts we make not to announce our business to the switchboard.' Then I go right into my introduction and work on establishing rapport."

This approach has been very successful for National Revenue.

How much authority is required to get through to the right party depends on the nature of your product. It is considerably more difficult in some fields than in others to break the ice and open new accounts. A purchasing agent with an electronics company may be highly receptive to a phone call from an electronic parts salesperson because the call is relevant to his work, and his success depends on knowing what's available. The same individual, however, might resent a call at the office from a life insurance salesperson, a stockbroker, a real estate agent, or an automobile salesperson regarding a personal matter rather than one that relates to his business. But this doesn't mean that these salespersons shouldn't call during office hours; in their field, nine to five represents prime selling time. If you maintain your conviction that what you have to offer is valuable to the person you're calling, you can project the necessary authority to get through to the right party no matter what you are selling.

LEAVING A MESSAGE

Leaving a message that works is an integral part of selling on the telephone. Often, you will not be able to get through to an individual on the first call, so it will be necessary for you to call back or to leave a message. There are messages, and *there are messages!*

Getting established accounts to return your calls should not be a problem. But leaving a message with a prospect is another story. What do you say to the secretary so that her boss, the president of the corporation, for example, will return your call? Some salespersons don't even try to leave a message, since their rate of return is so low. But others achieve excellent results, with up to 50 percent of their calls being returned. Obviously, they know techniques that increase the rate of returned calls. In this chapter, we will limit our discussion to leaving an effective message with a prospect you have never spoken to; because if this individual returns your call, you will certainly have no difficulty getting your clients to do the same.

The primary rule of leaving a message will probably sound familiar: *Speak with confidence and authority.* State your purpose in a pleasant and assertive manner. You must present yourself as an astute businessperson—which you are—and avoid saying anything that will type you as "just another salesman." The prospect, for instance, has probably had countless insurance agents call on him over the years. He probably believes himself to be satisfied with his present contacts. The odds are overwhelming that he did not wake up that morning with a sudden desire to hear from a new salesperson in your field. He may already have his sources. Therefore, unless your message projects confidence and authority to the person who takes the message, your call will probably not be returned.

You may end a telephone conversation with a screener by creating urgency, but you should do it indirectly. Instead of saying, "It's critical that Mr. Jones call me immediately," say something like, "Mention to Mr. Jones that if we can hear from him today, we'd appreciate it." A message like this creates urgency, but it's not artificial.

CALLING BACK

When an individual is difficult to reach and does not return your call, don't hesitate to call again. This time, ask the secretary her name, then *use* her name: "Susan, both Mr. Jones and I have very busy schedules. Is there any particular time when Mr. Jones might be more available? Is it in the morning or afternoon?" After her response, try to pinpoint a time by saying, "Susan, is two o'clock the best time, or would you suggest four o'clock?"

These specific questions also contribute to an air of businesslike firmness. The fact that you suggested two specific times implies that you do have a busy schedule. This leads her to think, He must be important if two o'clock and four o'clock are the only times today he can call. On the other hand, if you had simply asked when the prospect might be available, the question would suggest that you had nothing better to do with your time than to call at his convenience.

By way of contrast, notice how ineffectual it would sound to ask her, "Could you tell me when he might be free?" That question may lead her to answer, "No, I couldn't do that. He's very, very busy." In asking for the best time to call back, always be firm and specific.

Calling the secretary by her name is very important whether you are leaving a message or planning to call again. It's amazing, but 99 percent of the time she is treated as someone who is insignificant, a non-person. Most people do not call her by name. If you *do* have her name written down, and you must call a second or third time to reach the prospect, *use her name!* This will impress and influence her.

On the second call, your objective is not to leave another fruitless message. Therefore, you want to avoid having the screener say, "Don't call him, he'll call you." The air of authority and the suggestion that your own schedule is very hectic will help you avoid this. You are letting the screener know that you have something important to discuss with the prospect—but you will be the one to call back.

In some cases you may have to make a series of calls before you finally get through. You should call at least three times, and perhaps four. Remember, when a prospect is hard to reach, most other salespersons give up. The one who persists just might be the one who gets a substantial account.

When you do call the third time, the prospect may still be unavailable. In that case, you should once again emphasize to the screener that you wish to talk to the prospect. Now you should say something like "Susan, I have a very hectic schedule. It's going to be quite difficult for Mr. Jones to contact me. What do *you* think is the best time for me to contact him?" Once again, you are targeting the time to make the next call, but this time you are asking her to be your ally.

It's interesting to note how people are willing to help you when you ask them to. Once you feel comfortable with the rapport you have established with the screener, it is often very effective to ask her to do you a favor. "Susan, this is John Smith of United Corporation. I would sincerely appreciate it if you would tell me the best possible time to call Mr. Jones. What time this afternoon do you know for certain that I could get through to him?" You'll be surprised at how often a screener can be won over and will become eager to help you. It's human nature for people to want to do a favor—when you ask them at the right time, in the right way. This is especially true if you've laid the groundwork during your previous calls. You're addressing her by her first name, and she is in your corner. She *wants* you to get through. And remember, she has the authority to put you through to her boss.

If you have an assistant who is trained in getting through intermediaries, work closely with that person. Establish a system so that if there is any difficulty with the secretary on the wire, the call is turned over to you. This approach gives the salesperson an air of authority which is very effective. When the assistant's job is done properly, the salesperson's image is that of an important and authoritative individual. He will rarely fail to get through, because the stage has been set.

CONCLUSION

Nothing can be accomplished in telephone selling until you get through to the prospect. And it's essential that you talk to the *right* prospect—the decision-maker. Very often, you will encounter a barrier in the form of the telephone screener, whose job is to put through only those calls she deems important. Just how you handle the screener will very likely determine whether or not you are given an opportunity to speak with the prospect. Therefore, it's very important to project the image of a VIP, because the prospect's valuable time does not permit him to talk with insignificant callers.

There will always be some instances when you will have to make a series of calls before you finally get to talk directly with the prospect. In such cases, you must work on establishing rapport with the screener, while maintaining an image of authority.

Whether you leave a message after the first call or the fourth, leaving an effective message also requires authority and a quiet suggestion of urgency. All these techniques take practice, but developing them is an essential part of good telephone selling. Remember: *You must get through to the prospect before anything can be sold.*

4

The Initial Approach

Once you have finally made contact with the prospect, you must quickly arouse his interest to *keep* him on the telephone. After all, it's just as easy for him to quickly say, "I'm not interested. Good day, sir," as it is for his telephone screener. In fact, he is often more decisive in determining who is worthy of his time, so there's little reason to expect him to be shy about turning you down. He can hang up the receiver as quickly as he picked it up. But you do have one thing going for you now: the fact that his screener put you through has put the prospect in the proper frame of mind. He knows that only a small percentage get this far, so you must have something that the screener at least believes he will be interested in. The fact that he's paying to have his calls screened means that he values the screener's opinion!

LAYING THE GROUNDWORK

Even salespersons who give their major presentations on the phone rarely attempt to make a sale during the initial contact. This is particularly true where big-ticket items are involved. In the majority of cases, the initial call will soon be followed up by (1) a letter, (2) an in-person call, or (3) a telephone presentation. The first call, in other words, lays the groundwork for the presentation to come. Prior to making this call you must know your objective. To call haphazardly, without any specific plan, is futile.

Whether your intention on the first call is to make an appointment or to lay the groundwork for a future telephone presentation, it is vital to create the interest for keeping in touch. This paves the way for the transaction. You have already passed hurdle number one, the secretary. Because you have been effective in influencing her, you are connected with the prospect; and now you face hurdle number two—selling him on the idea of doing business with you. In this initial conversation, you are not only creating interest and rapport, you are laying the groundwork for an effective presentation.

GETTING YOUR FOOT IN THE DOOR

"Getting your foot in the door" is the first step in selling any product. If all prospects were immediately receptive to every salesperson, selling would be nothing more than taking orders. You must remember that, unlike the average customer who walks into a store, the cold-call prospect hasn't expressed an interest in the product. The need for your product may be the farthest thing from his mind. Therefore, the initial approach *has* to work or the sale can never be made. And if the other numbers are to work (so many calls equal so many sales), a salesperson needs a consistently effective approach. Without it, selling is a game of chance. Anyone can turn X percent out of every hundred calls into prospects; as the proverb goes, "Even a blind pig will stumble across some corn." But the skilled salesperson will convert one out of two or three cold calls into a solid prospect.

There are two ways to use the initial telephone call. One school of thought holds that the best use is to set up an appointment, without any attempt to sell. A second school believes in selling the product on the telephone, either during the initial call or at a later time when the prospect has been qualified. In general, the effectiveness of the method will depend on the nature of the product. For example, it is acceptable to sell products like stocks, bonds, and casualty insurance by telephone. But other products, including life insurance, computers, and real estate, are practically never sold directly by telephone. For products such as these, the telephone is valuable in setting up appointments with genuinely interested prospects. There are, of course, borderline products and services which are sold either way. It's a matter of the individual's preference. Whichever method you favor, this chapter will teach you how to make the initial approach that sets the foundation for a successful presentation.

Once you master the techniques of the initial approach, you will consistently get favorable results. Add good work habits to that, and you can set your production goals high—because the sky's the limit.

Bill Frankenstein, a Los Angeles life insurance agent, is a master at the techniques of the initial approach. Despite his success in the business, Bill still makes cold calls to a pre-selected list of prospects every Monday and Wednesday morning from eight-thirty to ten-thirty. "I call between thirty and fifty businesspersons," he says. "In person, I would only be able to reach five or six in the same amount of time. I enjoy making these calls, and it keeps me sharp. No matter how much success a life insurance agent has, he should never quit making cold calls. That's like a boxer who quits sparring. Those calls keep you in shape."

Some of Bill's appointments are also made by an assistant who works for him and two other agents. "We furnish him with a written presentation," Bill says, "and he does a good job for us."

Bill's telephone presentation is loaded with ways to create initial interest. A typical example would go like this:

"Mr. Smith, my name is Bill Frankenstein, and I'm with the Cambridge Group. I've been working with business people in the area, and I have some ideas I'd like to share with you. Is it okay if I ask you a few questions?"

Ninety percent of the prospects say yes at this point. Bill continues: "Are you happy with your life insurance program?"

The usual response to this is "Are you kidding? I'm insurance poor!" Variations include "Yes, I have a friend in the business," and "I can't afford any more insurance now."

Bill then replies, "John [he likes to get on a first name basis as soon as possible], I realize that. But if I could show you a way to reduce the cost of your insurance program by 50 to 60 percent and still maintain the same level of coverage, would you be interested?"

"How could you do that?"

"Well, it's not possible to convey by telephone. But I know you'll benefit by it. I expect to be in your area Tuesday and Thursday of next week. Which day is more convenient for you?"

Another way Bill creates interest is by asking, "If I could show you how to make your premiums tax deductible, would you be interested?" Or he might ask, "If I could show you how to have your present coverage paid for in eleven years, would you be interested?"

Bill is convinced that if a salesperson creates enough interest, no prospect is too busy to listen. "But you've got to get his attention," he emphasizes. "And I think the key to doing that is to have the attitude, 'I am going to help this client. He's not doing me a favor by listening to me. I'm doing him the favor.' *You can't be subservient.*" In other words, confidence and an air of authority are just as important in the initial approach as in getting through the screener.

Larry Schneider, a life insurance agent in Potomac, Maryland, also believes in the importance of creating quick initial interest. He starts his telephone presentation with an attention-getting statement: "Mr. Miller, my name is Larry Schneider, and I'm a premium maximizer." After a slight pause, the prospect inevitably asks, "What's a premium maximizer?"

Larry then goes into his telephone interview to set up an appointment. "Mr. Miller, if you're like other businessmen around here that I've helped, you're probably spending too much money on insurance and not getting a decent rate of return on your investment. You see, insurance is the biggest waste of money—until you have to use it. Then you wish you had more. If I could give you more for the same cost, or the same coverage for less cost, wouldn't you agree that would be terrific?

"I'm sure you agree that we should get together to discuss how we can accomplish this for you. Would next Tuesday at ten be convenient? Or I could see you on Wednesday in the early afternoon." (Notice how Larry, like other top salespersons, gives the prospect a *choice* of times—not "When would it be convenient?")

In the preceding examples, the one and only objective is to create enough initial interest to set up an appointment. With this in mind, the salesperson makes every attempt not to get into specifics on the telephone. The only result he seeks is the appointment. For this individual, the success of his telephone work is measured in the number of appointments he sets up. Either his personal style or his product or service demands that he sell in person. For him, trying to sell by phone would only create confusion and lead to failure. Nevertheless, in a very important sense, he *is* selling by phone—*selling the appointment.*

The sales representatives of National Revenue Corporation use a specific presentation for the initial approach. Their actual sales presentations must be made in person, since they use visual aids and review a prospect's receivables portfolio; however, they make about 50 percent of their appointments by phone.

Richard Schultz, the firm's president, stresses the importance of creating interest in that initial phone call. "I have to provide a reason for him to be interested in doing business with me," Richard says. "And basically, I do it by informing him that I will provide a return on his investment. What can be more important to a businessperson? But beyond stressing that fact, I avoid telling too much on the phone. If you give the prospect too much information, he will assume that he now knows enough to make a decision. Our prime objective is to make an appointment. When that is your goal, you can't allow the prospect to cross-examine you on the telephone so that he can make a hasty buying decision then and there."

In his first telephone conversation with a prospect, Richard creates initial interest through a number of statements. He begins by showing knowledgeability about the prospect's industry and by causing the prospect to wonder what his competitors may know that he does not.

"John, I'm working with members of the Hardware Association. We've been endorsed by the state association; and Sam Brown, the executive director, suggested I call you personally. Our company collects bad debts, and we do it a little differently than any other company in the country. We give a 100 percent guarantee on the results to our users, where, for an unusually low one-time fixed fee, we'll collect any account on your books. Now, John, this is regardless of the age, size, or the debtor's location—anywhere in the United States. And John, when you submit an account to us, we do all the work and the money is paid directly to your business.

"If the debtor won't pay, at your discretion we'll take him to court. Now, I know at times that can be firm, but that's why we get results. Now, I know if you're like most of the gentlemen I talk to in the hardware business, you probably have some accounts you'd like to turn into cash without spending that 33 to 50 percent in many cases to do so. Would that be correct in your case, John?" At this point, Richard waits for an affirmative reply. Then he continues: "Well, John, I'm going to be in your area tomorrow morning and back again on Thursday afternoon. I was wondering when might be the best time to catch you in, John?"

Richard gets his foot in the door by showing that his service is used by others in the prospect's industry. He creates interest by suggesting how much the prospect has to gain by using the service. But he does not supply enough information for the prospect to make a too-quick negative decision.

USING A THIRD PARTY AS AN INTRODUCTION

Ed Ellman, president of Ellman Financial and Service Corporation in Columbus, Ohio, frequently uses a third party referral, someone the prospect respects and relies on, when he calls a prospect. He may, for instance, call a client who is an important customer of the prospect and ask his client to mention that Ed Ellman will be calling. With this introduction, Ed is more than likely to be well received when he calls, since the prospect doesn't want to offend his good customer. And, like all salespersons, Ed wants a courteous prospect who is willing to hear him out.

The value of using a third party as an introduction is that it's an immediate endorsement; the prospect knows that you are reputable, reliable, knowledgeable, and deserving of his time. In the majority of cases, this alone is enough for a prospect to hear you out during your first telephone conversation with him. Then it's up to you to generate enough interest to set the stage for either your telephone sales presentation or an in-person meeting with him—whatever your goal might be.

QUALIFYING PROSPECTS

The primary purpose of qualifying prospects is to save time, so that the salesperson isn't calling on individuals who are not potential customers. Questions which help determine the prospect's ability to make a transaction also help the salesperson determine what product would be most useful.

Many professional salespersons have what is called "a warm-up session" with a prospect, in which they determine his needs. Such a session, typically involving a series of questions, serves a very useful purpose; not only do you learn what the prospect wants, but you also establish a relationship in which he is getting comfortable voicing his opinions. A life insurance agent, for instance, will ask such questions as How much life insurance do you carry at present? How did you arrive at that amount? What is your objective in obtaining additional insurance? And so on. A warm-up session is often part of a qualifying session, which will get into more detailed questions about the prospect's needs. In asking warm-up questions, the salesperson shows that he is different from the typical salesperson, whose interest may seem to be self-serving.

A stockbroker, for example, may begin by asking, "What are your objectives? What do you want to accomplish? Do you want investments that provide capital gains, or are you interested in income?" When a broker has an answer to that question, he may ask, "What investment have you made in the past several years that you consider to be the kind you're seeking now?" These questions help define exactly what the prospect's financial objectives are, so that the broker can help him reach them.

This kind of careful questioning is the mark of a professional.

After all, a doctor doesn't ask you, "Where does it hurt?" and then cut you open without further examination. A competent attorney will not recommend a course of action without getting all the facts. In the same way, the professional salesperson is marked by a careful attention to the prospect's needs.

In one way, selling yourself is an art, and salespersons who are adept at it often operate on their intuition. But it is also true that selling yourself boils down to a very basic rule: Show the customer that *you* are the person who can give him what he needs. *You* supply not just the product, but the right product; and *you* can be counted on for service. The best way in the world to demonstrate these facts is to qualify the customer properly.

The qualification process should never be rushed. Remember, you are getting to know the prospect, *and* you are demonstrating your professionalism. An experienced real estate agent does not expect to show homes after a five-minute chat with a couple. He must know the answers to such questions as What are their annual earnings? Do they have equity in their present home? If so, how much? What neighborhoods are they interested in? How large is the family? What are the ages of their children? Do they prefer older homes or newer homes? Do they like to garden? The questions go on and on. The answers will not only tell the agent what the couple needs, but the process will help build a relationship of trust.

Building rapport is a vital part of qualifying a prospect. The questions and answers *are* important—vitally important; without them, in most cases, you cannot supply the customer with the product he needs. But in addition to attaining valuable information, *proper qualifying helps you sell yourself.* It builds an aura of professionalism and sincerity. To return to the example of the real estate agent who may spend half an hour or more qualifying a couple, the wise agent knows that there is an army out there waiting to sell that couple the very same houses. The only thing any particular agent can offer that nobody else sells is himself.

Qualifying a client extends beyond the factual, qualifying questions. Most salespeople hope to have ongoing relationships with their clients. Accounts will be serviced; insurance policies will be increased; stocks will be bought and sold. Therefore it is desirable to continue to sell yourself by moving beyond the qualification questions into questions that will reveal the client as a person and help you build a relationship. In the long run, the most valuable commodity a salesperson can have is a relationship of friendly trust with a client. This cannot be gained in an artificial or insincere fashion. Great salespersons are characterized by their genuine interest in the people they do business with.

One approach which is often successful is to talk to the prospect on a personal basis about his own career. If you are genuinely interested, ask him how he achieved what he has. What ingredients got him there? What advice would he have for someone just starting out? While you're learning useful information about his company and his industry, you're also being given the basis on which to understand him as a person.

You cannot rush this kind of thing. It's important to realize that a personal relationship with a client is built up over a period of time and in stages. Many salespersons do it with a series of calls. The second or third time they talk to the prospect, they begin to ask more personal questions about his family, his hobbies, his recreation. A good salesperson is always interested in understanding what makes a client tick. Personal relationships build trust, and trust is the foundation for substantial future transactions and an ongoing relationship.

Relationships occur at different levels. Some people are more friendly and outgoing than others. They are completely open; they want to tell you about their personal lives. Others adhere strictly to business relationships. You have to accept this as the nature of the individuals. The fact that one client is at level one (indicating the highest rapport) and another is at level five (the lowest rapport) doesn't mean that one relationship is not as good as the other. Some people are very formal by nature; they don't open up with anyone. They may be introverted even with their best friends. They simply don't build rapport with anyone the way an outgoing person does, and you have to respect that. There is a world of difference in people. That doesn't mean your formal relationship with an introverted person is not every bit as good as your relationship with a more outgoing person.

THE FOLLOW-UP LETTER

Every salesperson must know how he will follow up the initial contact. It may be with a personal visit, a telephone presentation, a follow-up letter, or a combination of these approaches. You may send out a confirming letter *and* meet your prospect at the appointed time. Or you may call the prospect again to confirm the time for a personal meeting.

However you give your actual sales presentation, we recommend the follow-up letter as the most professional method of confirming an initial telephone conversation. The letter, which can also contain a brochure and your personal biosketch, gives the prospect something tangible and adds a new dimension to the relationship. If it is well done and really personalized, it will greatly enhance your image in his eyes. In addition, the letter may serve to remind the prospect of an agreement you arrived at in the initial call. That may be an agreement to meet at a certain time; or it may be a statement on his part that he would like to hear your ideas. Whatever your approach, a letter of this nature will consolidate your position with the prospect.

THE HARD-NOSED PROSPECT

Regardless of your product or service, you will from time to time encounter a tough prospect—one who is immediately hostile and rude. If you call on enough people, this is bound to happen. The only way to avoid it is not to make any cold calls at all—not a very good alternative. When you do come across this kind of person, remind yourself that prospects like this sometimes end up being the biggest accounts. Don't be intimidated by them. Be polite and sympathetic and persevere!

A great many salespeople make the mistake of immediately writing off a hostile prospect. But, despite his initial hostility, this prospect can often be sold. His defensive layer will frequently dissolve when a salesperson is polite and persistent. He might begin, for instance, by saying, "Another damned salesman! I've been pestered by five already today. I can't even do my work!"

In this case, your reply should show that you understand. "You know, you're absolutely right. That is a problem that we're being confronted with, too. I think it's a problem of not having quality salespeople to talk with." Rather than arguing, you have agreed with him, a very effective way to cool him down.

If you stick with the hostile person, he may very well get some steam off and then be so grateful for your understanding that he will do business with you. When that happens, he will be a loyal client, and you won't have to worry about losing the account—because it's unlikely that your competition will ever get through to him!

A certain percentage of the time, however, you will be unable to make any progress with him. When he hangs up on you, you must have the attitude that you're satisfied that it worked out that way. After all, he let you know his position immediately. Instead of wasting a lot of time with the prospect, you only lost a few minutes. Remind yourself of the mathematical formula: X number of calls results in Y amount of business. The unpleasant person is part of that formula; he must be there in order for you to succeed. He is one more completion, which brings you that much closer to your next sale.

CONCLUSION

Getting through the telephone screener can be tough, and may in itself seem like a real achievement; but unless your initial approach to the prospect is effective, nothing has been gained. Once you get your foot in the door, the real selling begins. You must attract the prospect's attention by creating an interest, and just how well you accomplish this depends on the image you convey. Remember, you get only one chance to make a first impression. Make sure it's a good one.

In addition to selling yourself during the initial approach, you must often do a certain amount of qualifying in order to determine whether or not you can be of service to the prospect. Don't hesitate to ask a lot of questions. Not only is this warm-up session necessary if you are to serve him, but when properly carried out, it creates an air of professionalism. It also shows him that you sincerely care about his welfare—you're not just interested in a fat commission check. The qualifying process is often an ideal time to get to know your prospect and begin establishing a relationship of mutual trust. A follow-up letter after your initial approach is also highly professional, and an excellent way to confirm a telephone conversation.

Finally, don't shy away from the prospect who initially gives you resistance. If you remain calm and courteous, he may become a valuable account. And if you don't get through to him, remember that it's all part of the business. You can't realistically expect to generate a sale from every prospect you talk to!

5

The Telephone Presentation

Now that you've captured the prospect's attention—he's on the other end of the wire and available to have a conversation with you —the time has come to make your presentation. Obviously this is the "meat" of the entire selling process. During this conversation you will inform him about such things as your company, your product, and yourself, as well as the reasons he should buy your product. This must be done in a well-organized and interesting manner. If you do it haphazardly, you will quickly confuse the prospect and lose his respect, and your chances of generating business with him will be greatly diminished. There's more to making a telephone presentation than simply picking up the receiver and having a bull session with a prospect. No matter how many people have told you that you have a great personality, you can't rely on it to carry a sale. You must have a good presentation!

THE PLANNED PRESENTATION

Every salesperson eventually has a planned presentation—regardless of whether he originally intended to or not. Over a period of time, through trial and error, a "best" way to present the product evolves. Whether a salesperson realizes it or not, he is soon giving practically identical presentations to every prospect. Since this is true, why not deliberately *plan* your presentation? Why risk having it develop without careful thought or direction? Arriving at a presentation through trial and error means the loss of many sales.

If you head a sales organization, you will want your representatives to present the product with some degree of uniformity. Certainly you will want to give new salespeople the advantage of having the best possible presentation. Thorough training with a proven presentation holds turnover to a minimum. Without a tested presentation, some salespeople are never able to develop effective presentations of their own. Others become discouraged and fall by the wayside. It's no wonder that most professional sales organizations now provide their people with a carefully developed presentation, and training in how to deliver it.

The prepared presentation can simply be a track to follow, or it can be a script that is delivered verbatim. People who have never worked with a carefully planned presentation often react to the idea by saying that a memorized sales talk sounds "canned." What's worse, if you're interrupted, you have trouble getting back on the track. But that's where the difference between a professional and a non-professional becomes obvious. The professional salesperson knows his presentation so well that it doesn't sound canned. And because he has practiced it until he is letter-perfect, he will not be thrown off the track with interruptions and distractions.

There are many other excellent reasons for using a planned presentation. For one thing, when you do, all the facts are fully covered every time; nothing is inadvertently omitted. Furthermore, bad habits are minimized. The salesperson who uses a planned presentation does not talk his way past the close, or pause too long at a crucial moment in search of the right word. Another significant benefit is that knowing what you are going to say, and knowing that it works, gives confidence—an absolutely essential ingredient in selling.

A planned presentation also enables you to work yourself out of a selling slump. Let's face it, even the best of us have our bad periods. But the salesperson who doesn't have a prepared sales presentation—the one who says something different to each prospect—doesn't have any way of knowing what he said wrong! With a prepared sales presentation, on the other hand, it's considerably easier to review yourself, find out where you went off the track, and put yourself back on it again.

It takes many hours to develop a good planned presentation. But the advantage is tremendous. Such a presentation provides a way to inform the prospect without confusing him. It is clear, concise, and easy to follow. And remember that a confused person has difficulty making a buying decision. Instead, he hems and haws, feeling incapable of making a decision that involves money. The easiest thing for him to do is procrastinate—delay the transaction. But a good presentation is designed to make it easy for the prospect to buy. It gives him a step-by-step method by which he can obtain your product or service.

Perhaps more than anything else, a planned presentation gives you direction. The exact route to your destination has been carefully considered and mapped out. Without this map, you can easily be sidetracked by objections and lose your sense of purpose. With it, everything you say helps get you to the destination; each sales point complements the others. You have seen to it that you have all the ammunition you will need to persuade the other party to act. When you have worked out your presentation carefully and practiced it until you can deliver it well, you have programmed yourself to succeed!

KNOWING YOUR PRODUCT

In a telephone sales presentation, you always have the advantage over the individual you are calling, because you can be prepared in advance. *You* are the expert. You have given a great deal of thought to the conversation that is to follow. You have more knowledge about your product and company, and about the competition, than he does—if you do your homework.

As you prepare a presentation, the first point you should consider is your product or service. You must tell what it is and how it works. You must also explain how it is superior to what the competition offers. In general, the story about the product should be as clear as possible, but don't make it complicated. As Joe Girard, who is the all-time greatest automobile salesman, says, "Most salesmen bore a guy to death when they start to talk about the technical details. I've seen salesmen sell a car and then buy it back. I watch these guys and I say to myself, 'He's got the car sold, but he won't stop talking.' "

Of course, the product information is extremely important; it's the heart of your presentation. But you must remember that simply educating the prospect is not enough. You aren't paid to pass on information. You're paid to produce sales. So, while the product story is vital, you should design your presentation to create the desire for action. Remember, it's great to tell—but you're paid to sell!

BUILDING A GOOD PRESENTATION

The basic element of every good presentation is a philosophy. When a prospect says, "If you're selling real estate, I'm not interested," or "I don't talk to insurance agents," or "I've got a stockbroker already," the top salesperson is not intimidated. A universal characteristic of great salespersons is that they do not perceive themselves as people who simply purvey a product such as insurance or stocks. They see themselves as professionals who offer something unique.

These professionals have a basic philosophy that they believe can meet the needs of the prospect. They have a potential way of building wealth or creating personal satisfaction. The product is the practical vehicle that attains the results. The concept is the motivating force that seeks out the product. A concept, or basic philosophy, is an inspirational force that allows a salesperson to communicate on a level unattainable by those who lack it. In other words, a super salesperson is not product-centered; he is concept-centered.

A stockbroker with a strong philosophy about investment might say, for example, "One way to take advantage of high interest rates is to invest in a company where the dividend is not reduced if interest rates come down." Note that this is not a statement about a specific stock, but an overall strategy. Likewise, any insurance agent worth his salt is aware of prospects who have never given much thought to the question of life insurance and have no philosophy about it. They're referred to as non-believers. The agent must demonstrate to them what the policy benefits will do; he must in a sense create their need through giving his own philosophy about life insurance.

A life insurance agent's philosophy may be that a life insurance policy is the only absolute way to guarantee an individual's estate the necessary funds to provide for his widow and surviving children. He may believe that there is no other means of creating X amount of dollars immediately, the first day the policy is in force. This philosophy will be apparent in his presentation: "Mr. Brown, how else can you create an estate of $500,000 in the event of your untimely death, say tomorrow, with an initial investment of $10,-000? Sure, you can invest your money yearly in real estate, and *if* you live long enough, you will receive a greater return than a life insurance policy will provide. But what happens if you die in the meantime? How will your family then be provided for? An immediate estate of $500,000 can only be guaranteed through a life insurance policy."

A real estate agent may believe real estate to be the best all-around hedge against inflation. This philosophy must be part of his presentation. "The rising values of real estate have traditionally been the best hedge against inflation. Regardless of how high today's prices may seem to you, they'll appear to be bargain prices in the not-too-distant future. There will always be a demand for home ownership, and the supply of premium locations will never increase. And, with construction costs skyrocketing, new construction will cost considerably more in the future than it does today. I am absolutely convinced that we can expect real estate values to continue to spiral for many years to come—at the very least for the remainder of our lifetimes."

The salesperson who possesses a strong basic philosophy will be able to overcome difficult situations. For instance, a secretary may say, "If you're calling in reference to selling stocks, Mr. Jones has a broker." The top salesperson is not discouraged to hear this, because he does not think of himself as a broker selling products anyone can sell. He is a professional with a philosophy about investing. And he is not calling to sell stocks, but to make a judgment as to the needs of the prospect and whether the prospect qualifies for his services. The broker with a philosophy is a professional, operating in a large arena. A broker without a basic philosophy, however, may see himself as merely an order-taker.

Every field is dominated by non-professionals who have no particular philosophy about their selling. They limit themselves to selling a specific product instead of using the product as a means for the prospect to attain broader objectives. Without this overview, the salesperson's product knowledge is diluted; his presentation lacks the conviction of a true believer. He will stumble in the initial approach, and his lack of a real philosophy will be quite obvious in the presentation. However, the salesperson who sells a *concept* projects unmistakable conviction.

Bob Knowlton, vice president of Security Pacific Mortgage Company, always approaches a new prospect with an idea rather than a product. Bob calls on builders and developers in the residential real estate market throughout the Denver area, and his policy is to try to sell a new product first to the biggest, most successful builder in the area. "If I can knock down the biggest builder first," he says, "the rest come easy."

When a sales strategy dictates beginning with a crucial top person in a field, the initial approach has to be good. Bob successfully makes appointments with an approach that stresses the *idea*. "One of the best ways of prospecting," he says, "is by saying to the individual, 'Our company has come up with a new idea I think you'll be interested in, and we would like to discuss it with you.' In my twenty-five years in business, very few people have ever turned me down." In his presentation, as well as his initial approach, Bob very successfully stresses the concept before he presents the specific product.

An equally vital element of the presentation is *conviction*. While you will probably not say to the prospect, "You need this product and I know it," your presentation should convey that message. It's a *good* product or service, the best value of its kind. If you've done your homework, you know your product and you know why it is good. And *you* are the best person to buy the product from. Your conviction will come through in your voice, as well as in such phrases as "an extraordinary opportunity" and "a tremendous value."

If you lack conviction, your presentation will seem insincere and will not be believable. If you can't manufacture conviction for what you're selling, perhaps you're in the wrong field, because without conviction you'll never rise above mediocrity.

A good presentation will always create *urgency.* The stockbroker, the life insurance agent, the real estate agent, can all state with conviction, "I think you would agree with me that in anything we do, timing is critical." Of course, the urgency must not be artificial but should be solidly based on facts.

Pointing out the importance of timing helps the prospect see the need for a decision. It's a natural human tendency to put off making a decision, particularly when a large sum of money is in question. People would prefer to think it over, and may make any number of objections indicating their indecisiveness. Only with faith in your product and solid knowledge can you create a sense of urgency, so that the prospect sees it is to his advantage to act —now!

One way to create this urgency is to make the prospect realize the actual dollar savings he will have if he makes an immediate decision. If he puts off his buying decision, for instance, the price of a house may increase; the price of a particular stock may rise. You can also create urgency if the product is one that will not always be available. A house may be purchased by another interested party; an automobile may be sold, and there are no more like it in inventory. The list of urgent reasons to buy is endless, and the reasons will vary from one industry to another. But whatever the statements used to create urgency, they must be grounded in fact and expressed with conviction.

Another key ingredient in a good presentation is *personal communication.* A successful presentation involves more than product knowledge, philosophy, conviction, and urgency. It requires a personal understanding of the prospect's needs. What are his real plans for himself and his family? What does he intend to do in the next five years to reach his financial goals? How can the two of you work together to ensure his success? If he considers you his friend, as well as a conscientious and knowledgeable person, your working relationship with him will become a lifetime one. So get to know your prospect on a personal basis. Your business associates can also be your friends.

Once you have prepared a presentation, go back over it several times, asking yourself whether it has the basic elements. Does it convey urgency? Can you point out phrases and sentences that show conviction? Is the philosophy clear? Is the product story presented briefly and convincingly? Have you included personal communication? If you can answer yes to all these questions, you have developed a good presentation.

STRUCTURING THE PRESENTATION

A presentation has an introduction, a body, and a close. It is important that these parts receive the appropriate emphasis. Most salespersons take a considerable amount of time in their introduction and presentation of the product and buying reasons. Often the body of the presentation is so long that they fail to close. If they do reach the close, the issue has been belabored for so long that the prospect just wants to get off the phone. It's not that these salespersons don't present good buying reasons or include the right ingredients; it just boils down to structuring the presentation poorly. They get bogged down in the middle. Remember that *the most important part of a presentation is the close.*

Suppose your average conversation with a prospect is twenty minutes. Instead of having a four-minute introduction, a fourteen-minute presentation, and a two-minute close, change things around. Your introduction can be brief, perhaps two minutes. If you have already spoken once to the prospect and sent him a follow-up letter, as we recommended, he knows you and your company. The body of the presentation should then take four to six minutes, no more, and the remaining twelve to fourteen minutes should be spent on the close. In other words, most of the presentation should be spent asking for the order.

It is certainly possible that in four to six minutes you will not present all the benefits of the product. Instead, you will present further benefits as you overcome objections. Each time you do, you will ask for the order again.

The average busy person begins to get impatient after fifteen or twenty minutes on the telephone, and sometimes sooner. This structure allows you to get immediately to the heart of the presentation—asking for the order. In four or six minutes, you have given three or four good buying reasons. It is not necessary to overwhelm the prospect with every possible buying reason. He may be ready to buy now. Find out. If he is not, present additional reasons and close again. You will be able to do this if the presentation is structured properly so that most of the time is allotted to asking for the order.

As you can see, overcoming objections and closing will be an integral part of your basic presentation. Therefore, your presentation should not be written until you have studied the techniques given in Chapter 6, "How to Handle Every Objection Ever Made," and Chapter 7, "Closing the Sale." Your own rebuttals to objections and your own methods of asking for the order can then be made an integral part of your planned presentation.

THE DELIVERY

In delivering his presentation, the telephone salesperson has an advantage over the person who sells face to face. The latter must have his presentation memorized; but the telephone salesperson can work from his notes. For anyone with a poor memory, this is a distinct advantage and saves a great deal of work. And not only can you have the presentation in front of you, but you can have your data bank (the file card with relevant information about the prospect) at your fingertips. With a little practice, you can learn to use these resources so that the impression you create is that of a knowledgeable professional.

Many salespeople, however, still prefer to learn their telephone presentations verbatim. National Revenue's Richard Schultz firmly believes that only a salesperson with a preprogrammed presentation can think on his feet and meet any objection. "You go through three stages of learning," he explains. "First is what I call 'conscious incompetence,' when you're brand new, you're trying to learn, and you know you're not doing it very well. It's like when you were a kid, trying to tie your shoes. You had to think about it every time you did it, and half the time you did it wrong.

"Pretty soon you get good—you could tie a bow most of the time —but you still had to think about it. That's 'conscious competence,' the second stage. Finally, with enough practice, you reach the third stage, which I refer to as 'unconscious competence.' You can tie your shoes now without even thinking about it at all. Well, when a salesperson can give his telephone presentation by heart so well that he doesn't even have to think about it, his mind is free to watch for buying signals, to control the interview.

"When you have unconscious competence, the prospect can ask you anything and you won't be thrown off on a tangent. You can plan and replan your sales strategy while you talk. Unconscious competence is truly amazing. For instance, if you say the alphabet as fast as you can, it will probably take you less than four seconds. And all the while you're doing it, you can think about something else. But try saying it every other letter: A, C, E, and so on. It takes much longer. You can do it, but you're not programmed. It's *conscious* competence. And your mind is not free to think of anything else.

"When a salesperson knows his presentation so well that he's delivering it with unconscious competence, he really has a decisive edge," Richard emphasizes. "There is no objection the prospect can make that he can't answer. In the case of a seasoned salesperson, he's heard that objection a thousand times, and he automatically gives the perfect reply. And in the case of a well-trained novice, he can say, 'Well, Howard, that's why I called,' and turn the objection around to his advantage. At the very least, he can get smoothly back into his presentation, because he knows it so well."

Whether or not you memorize your presentation verbatim, you will need to practice it. As the old saying goes, "It's not what you say, it's how you say it." Nowhere is this truer than in sales. The best presentation in the world will fail if it sounds canned. And it will sound canned, whether you read it or memorize it, unless you practice, practice, practice.

Experienced salespeople recommend practicing with a tape recorder, and large sales organizations often tape a presentation as the first step in diagnosing weaknesses. Richard Schultz reports that frequently a salesperson who records his own presentation will come back with the word that he doesn't need any help critiquing it—it's obvious now what he's doing wrong. And there's no reason why you can't tape-record an actual presentation on the telephone with another salesperson acting as the prospect. It helps pin down the weak points.

A good salesperson never really stops refining a presentation, although he may know it so well he could almost do it in his sleep. There are those who refuse to work carefully on a presentation because they believe it will lose its spontaneity. But nothing could be further from the truth. Some people can speak off the cuff and their material still sounds "canned." But a good professional can give his presentation thousands of times verbatim and nobody will ever detect that every word is memorized.

CONTROLLING THE PRESENTATION

In many ways a sales presentation is like a performance. Just as an actor's success is measured by applause, your success is measured by the prospect's response. And just as a good actor has the audience "in the palm of his hand," a professional salesperson holds his client's attention. When an actor loses control, the audience may be bored and restless, may hiss or boo, and may even walk out. Likewise, the salesperson who loses control of the telephone conversation will lose his audience. The prospect doesn't have to walk out—he just says no and hangs up!

To reach your objective and create a transaction, you must guide the conversation with the prospect. In effect, you take him step by step through your presentation, looking for the end result to be a sale. Guiding that conversation so that it reaches your destination is essential. If you fail to control it, the odds are that the sale will be lost.

On the surface, controlling the interview seems easier in face-to-face selling than over the telephone, and to many salespersons it probably is. They will argue that you can capture a prospect's attention more easily when he's sitting across the desk from you than over the telephone. Then, too, physical appearance can make it more difficult for the prospect to abruptly end a presentation, especially if he's five foot five and you happen to be six foot three! But those advantages of face-to-face selling are only superficial. By rehearsing a telephone sales presentation, you can refine it to the degree where every word you say will have your prospect literally sitting on the edge of his chair listening to you. With proper delivery—varying your rate of speech, raising and lowering your voice at the right times—and with a presentation that spells out what to say and when to say it, you will control the telephone conversation with the same ease as if you were there in person. In fact, on the telephone a prospect has to concentrate harder to hear what you have to say, and by doing this he tends to block out all physical distractions, thus giving you his undivided attention. But remember, you won't hold his attention for long unless you deliver a superior presentation.

It is during the delivery that the advantage of a carefully prepared presentation becomes obvious. *You* know exactly how to direct the conversation, because you are following a track; and *you,* not the prospect, know where it is going. You're following a road map, and he's coming right along, following you. As you can see, this gives you complete control of the presentation!

CONCLUSION

A well-prepared sales presentation is a necessity in telephone selling. It gives you direction, and it gives you full control of the conversation. It also prevents you from becoming sidetracked. Furthermore, it's relatively easy to review a planned presentation whenever you're in a sales slump and thereby put yourself back on track. You know your presentation works; after all, it's a proven thing. So once you've mastered it, it's simply a matter of relying on the law of averages and making enough calls. Your proven presentation guarantees that you will get favorable results.

A good presentation is not arrived at haphazardly but is planned and refined. While it shows your complete, professional knowledge of the product or service you sell, a good presentation does not merely inform. It also presents the philosophy that makes you more than "just a salesman," and it presents that philosophy with conviction. It creates urgency, and it leaves room for personal communication with the prospect. Whether it is read or memorized, a good presentation sounds spontaneous and sincere.

Highly successful salespersons sound natural when giving their telephone presentations. It's often hard to believe that they have had to work hard to arrive at such an outstanding delivery. But, as everyone must, they have paid a price for success. A novice who watches a professional salesperson at work is like a non-golfer at the Masters Tournament. The pros swing that club so easily! "It's so natural!" But experienced golfers know there's nothing natural about a golf swing. It's mechanical and must be learned—as the beginner quickly discovers when he addresses a golf ball for the first time! Through practice, however, he too can develop a "natural" swing. Likewise, any conscientious salesperson can develop an effective presentation and learn to deliver it in a natural and convincing manner. The salesperson who is willing to put in the time and effort can count on one day receiving the ultimate compliment from someone who doesn't know there's no such thing as a born salesman: "It's easy for you. You're a born salesman!"

6

How to Handle
Every Objection
Ever Made

The majority of novice salespersons interpret an objection as a rejection—the prospect decided not to buy. Since they have a built-in fear of rejection, they simply stop selling. The professional salesperson does not welcome rejection either, but he has an entirely different attitude toward objections. To him, an objection does not mean "No," but rather "I'm not convinced yet. Give me a more compelling reason to buy." Therefore, rather than reacting negatively, he welcomes the objection as an opportunity. He will continue to sell and refuse to be discouraged. He knows that's what makes him a successful salesperson. If he didn't have to deal with objections, he would simply be an order taker!

Top salespersons point out that most of their sales are closed *after* the prospect has expressed objections. Putting it another way, unsuccessful salespersons lose more sales than they make, because they have not learned the art of handling objections. In the great majority of cases, an objection is not a refusal but rather a request for additional information. The sale does not terminate when an objection is voiced. On the contrary, this is where real selling begins. A challenge has been presented. The prospect has shown that he does not fully recognize the value you are offering and that he's not ready to buy. If you want to create a transaction, you must show him why he should buy.

In answering objections, the telephone salesperson must have highly developed skill and sensitivity. For one thing, it is easier for a prospect to say no over the telephone than when a salesperson is sitting across from him. All he has to do is say, "Look, I'm not interested. And I can't talk any further because someone just walked into my office. Thank you for calling. Good-bye." In a face-to-face presentation, on the other hand, the prospect still has to confront the salesperson eyeball to eyeball after an objection like that. He can't break the connection and have the salesperson disappear.

Other factors also influence your handling of objections over the telephone. The telephone salesperson does not have the benefit of the visual signals that often show that an objection is false. He can't see the blush that may accompany an incorrect statement. Nor can he observe the prospect fidgeting or tapping his fingers on the desk. These visual clues would clearly signal "I don't really mean that. I'm simply not convinced yet."

On the plus side, the telephone salesperson will be making many more presentations in his selling time. That alone makes up for the lack of visual cues. In addition, he can develop sensitivity to the prospect's tone of voice, pauses, emphasis, and the conviction with which the prospect makes the objection. But most important, he must assume that the individual who makes an objection has simply not been properly convinced—and he must press on. Every professional salesperson knows that the sale does not really begin until the prospect says no—and he refuses to let objections defeat him. He knows this attitude is what separates the professional from the novice.

OBJECTIONS AS DEFENSE MECHANISMS

Every salesperson must realize early in his career that the vast majority of prospects approach a sales presentation with built-in defense mechanisms. In addition to environmental, air, water, and noise pollution, the prospect has probably been subjected to *telephone pollution.* Over a period of years, he has been bombarded with non-professional solicitation on the telephone, both as a consumer and as a businessperson. The volume of this solicitation makes it impossible for him to consent to listen to every presentation, let alone buy every product or service being offered.

Because of this, the typical prospect automatically assumes the position that he will say no to the request for the transaction. After all, he has only a limited amount of yeses, and saying yes to one request means giving up cash that would otherwise be available for something else. Perhaps he has recently been asked to purchase a large life insurance policy, a summer home, or a block of stock in what appears to be an undervalued company. He may be thinking of buying a new car or a boat. His wife has been talking about a mink coat. Or he'd like to put additional capital into his expanding business. He is fully cognizant of the fact that he can't say yes to all the opportunities that come his way—even if they all represent good values. He simply does not have the purchasing capacity! Therefore, he is preconditioned to say no.

You must understand this, however, and remember that he reacts this way toward most products and services that are offered him. He has built up a strong resistance to all sales presentations. The resistance is not aimed at you particularly but is his standard reaction to salespersons. This should not discourage you. He *can* be sold, but you must first overcome his defense mechanism.

The prospect gives you the opportunity to do that when he makes an objection. The fact that he is giving you feedback, and is still on the phone waiting to hear what you have to say, means that he is not rejecting the product but requesting more information. He is not convinced that one of his limited number of yeses should be granted to your offer. In effect, he is telling you, "Look, Mr. Salesman. You haven't convinced me. Your story wasn't strong enough. If you give up now, that will show me that I was right to think I didn't need what you're selling. But if you have enough conviction that I should buy it, then keep right on selling, because I can still be sold!"

The salesperson now has the opportunity to re-evaluate his strategy. Perhaps his philosophy wasn't strong enough. He may not have developed enough of a rapport with his prospect. Maybe there wasn't enough urgency in the presentation; the prospect doesn't see any need to take immediate action. The salesperson has not pressed the right button, the one that would make the prospect eager to make the purchase.

THE RIGHT ATTITUDE

To be successful, a salesperson must have the idea deeply ingrained in his mind that *every prospect is a potential customer*. No matter how strong and firm an objection may seem to be, you must continue to believe that this sale can be consummated. We have stressed that concept throughout this book. In every single aspect of selling, from the initial approach to the close, you must always believe that the sale can be consummated. But, although this attitude is important throughout the entire selling process, at no time is it more important than when you are "on the firing line" handling objections.

Of course, "you can't sell 'em all." Every salesperson must remember that, and use it to shrug off unsuccessful calls. At the same time, in approaching each individual presentation you must tell yourself that you *will* make the sale. And no matter what objections the prospect may make, you cannot allow yourself to think otherwise. Remember, most sales are closed *after* the objections have been expressed. Obviously, your success as a salesperson depends on your ability to overcome such obstacles. In the majority of your sales presentations, you will encounter some resistance. If you begin to have doubts when this happens, you will forfeit a substantial percentage of your sales. So bear in mind that every prospect can be sold—if you handle his objections correctly.

When, despite your best efforts, you can't close the sale, accept that as part of the business, and approach the next prospect with the same positive attitude. Above all, never let the resistance of one prospect carry over and dampen your confidence on the next call. You must be able to continue with your next call with the same degree of enthusiasm as if you had just successfully closed a sale.

REAL OBJECTIONS VERSUS FALSE OBJECTIONS

Whenever possible, establish your prospect's real reason for not making a buying decision. Until you know the real objection, you can't counter it. For instance, a prospect may say that his budget won't permit him to purchase additional merchandise at this time. However, his real reason for not buying is that his partner must be consulted. Previously, for reasons of pride, he has implied that he has total authority. Now he is not willing to tell you that he cannot make a decision alone. No matter how much you counter his stated objection, attempting to convince him that he can't afford not to add your merchandise to his inventory, you won't get anywhere, because you aren't touching the real objection. Without knowing a prospect's real objection, it is highly unlikely that you will convince him to change his mind, because your selling points are not related to the actual issue at hand.

In many cases, a prospect will voice an objection without being aware himself of what his real objection is. Often, he simply rejects buying decisions by reflex. Frequently this type of prospect will make a string of unrelated objections. No sooner do you answer one than he has another, and he believes they are real objections. He may begin with "Send me some literature. I want to read up on it." After you have answered this objection, he retorts with "I have to talk it over with my wife." That is followed by "Let me review my savings accounts." No matter how thoroughly you answer his objection, he has another one waiting in the wings. This prospect just doesn't want to make a decision. Answering his false objections will probably not convince him.

A series of unrelated objections should always be seen as excuses for not buying. Nobody could possibly have so many different real reasons for putting off a decision. Such a prospect is stalling, and is probably capable of inventing objections all afternoon. Your task is to find out by gentle probing how to overcome his hesitancy. What would it take to persuade him to buy? One good way to do this is to repeat your presentation, using a slightly different format.

By listening to his reactions, you will eventually find his "hot button."

Real or false, objections are natural and they should be expected. They are part of the selling process, and must be dealt with. In time, every professional salesperson gets to know which objections are probably false and should not be taken at face value: "I want to think it over." "I want to compare your prices with some other companies'." "I never make a decision on the spur of the moment." These statements may very well be clues that the prospect simply is not convinced yet. It is important not to be discouraged by this fact. The objection is part of a dialogue, and it gives you the opportunity to counter it. But it can be a serious mistake to take every objection at face value. For example, if you consent to call back every prospect who says, "Sounds interesting. Give me a call in a few days," your chances of survival as a salesperson will be greatly diminished.

The basis of most false objections is the fact that a large percentage of people resist *any* decision-making. Usually the reason for this is that deciding is risky. They might make the wrong decision, and they'd rather play safe and do nothing at all! But they also realize that decisions are necessary. It's your job to convince them that by not acting they will be making a decision that can work against them. They are often aware of their inability to take what they know is the right action, and although they seem to resist, they may really want your help in making a wise purchase. As a professional salesperson, it's your job to show them how to make an affirmative buying decision. The salesperson who gives up when he encounters initial resistance and false objections is doing his customer a disservice. In such cases, both the customer and the salesperson lose out.

BEING DIPLOMATIC

Every objection, real or unreal, must be treated with respect and diplomacy. Although the prospect may be employing his defensive mechanisms, he is probably not even aware of why he is resisting you, and his objections must be taken as seriously as if they were real. There is no such thing as an unworthy objection. Unfortunately, some salespersons react arrogantly to objections they believe are false. Rather than attempting to understand what the prospect is really saying, they will demolish the objection with some such remark as "That just doesn't make sense." This kind of know-it-all talk is counterproductive. One must always remember that *the objective is not to overcome all the objections; the objective is to close the sale.*

In handling objections, you must always be sympathetic to the needs of the prospect. Overcoming objections is a delicate procedure which requires intelligence. It must be done in such a way that the prospect feels comfortable with the removal of his objections. It is useless to remove an objection if you do it in such a way that the prospect resents you. He must want to do business with you not only because you know your product but because of your sincere desire to help him. In addition to his needing what you sell, it's important that he likes you.

Objections should be handled tactfully but directly. Whatever the objection may be, take it seriously and meet it head-on. But be careful to empathize with the prospect and respect his way of thinking. For example, a prospect may tell a stockbroker that he can't afford to buy at this time. He may go into detail: "I'm building a second home now, and it's going to take a lot of money." Although the broker takes the objection seriously, he must analyze it. Is this the real reason? Could the prospect make the investment? In the majority of cases, the answer is yes.

The broker should begin tactfully by agreeing with the prospect. "Fine. I can understand how you think about this." Then, after a slight pause he can add, "In these inflationary times it's very difficult to save. Therefore I think the savings feature of this issue is significant. It could add to your net worth. If you look ahead five years, it's possible that this investment will increase your standard of living." Although the broker understands that the prospect's objection may only be part of his reason for being hesitant, nevertheless, the broker answers the objection directly.

In responding to objections, a salesperson must be sensitive to the danger of being too dominant. It's always possible that the prospect will interpret a salesperson's control of the conversation as domineering. To prevent this, the prospect should be invited into the conversation. When an objection is answered, the salesperson should conclude with a statement that asks for the prospect's consent. A stockbroker might say, for instance, "You do agree with me that the company's growth rate of 20 percent is impressive, considering the industry's performance?" Then the prospect must be given time to answer.

"And would you agree that such a company should command a higher premium than the average multiple in the industry? That makes sense to you, doesn't it?" The broker is creating agreement with these questions, as well as drawing the prospect into the conversation. First he agrees with the prospect, then he gives the prospect the opportunity to agree with him.

Most important, objections should never be answered in a hostile manner. You don't want to spend twenty minutes overcoming objections only to find that the prospect feels intimidated, and you end up losing the sale. Your purpose is to create a transaction, not to "win the conversation." When a salesperson does that, he may have answered all the objections, but he has achieved nothing.

ANSWER THE OBJECTION AND CLOSE THE SALE

As we pointed out earlier, the professional salesperson expects objections and sees them as opportunities to close the sale. Once you answer an objection, you should always ask for the order again. You must do this as automatically as if the prospect had actually said to you, "Tell me why I should buy right now, and I will." When you have answered an objection diplomatically and intelligently, it is time to see if he is ready now to create the transaction. In many cases you will be faced with a series of objections. When that happens, don't hesitate to attempt to close the sale after you answer each objection.

While closing techniques will be treated fully in the next chapter, it is appropriate to mention here our rule of thumb: *Request the order three times.* After each objection, present the prospect with a complete explanation—and request the order. The salesperson who asks for the order three times will be far more successful than the one who makes only one request. Studies have shown that when three requests are made instead of one, productivity can increase fivefold. Beyond the third request, the law of diminishing returns will probably set in. This, however, does not mean you should not attempt additional closes, if you sense that they may be productive.

When you have answered several objections and closed three times, one good technique is to say, "Bill, do I understand you correctly, that this is your only reason for not buying? Is it correct to say that everything else makes sense to you if it were not for . . ." State the prospect's objection. Then pause. Your silence is very important at this stage.

Once he has agreed, you continue by repeating his objection, and adding, "Well, that is a tough one, and I can understand why that's your reason for not buying at this time. But I'm going to demonstrate how your doubts can be resolved."

At this point, your prospect has made an indirect commitment. He has agreed to limit his objection to one single point. Now you give him a complete, clear-cut explanation that refutes his only objection. It goes without saying that you immediately assume the sale and ask for the order following your reply. This technique works well when you can isolate one objection and have the prospect commit himself to making a decision if you can satisfy that last objection.

HOW TO HANDLE SPECIFIC OBJECTIONS

Since it would be impossible to list every objection the human mind could invent, we are limiting ourselves to handling several key objections. Most are general in nature. Regardless of the product being sold in the examples, every salesperson can apply the *principles* in handling objections in his own field. Answering objections does not require a repertoire of dozens of rebuttals; a handful of strong all-purpose answers will be applicable to almost every situation. It's up to you to control the sales interview and use these principles to meet every objection head-on with your own most appropriate rebuttal.

- "Not today."
- "I want to think it over."
- "Send me some literature."
- "I never make up my mind on a salesperson's first call."
- "I want to discuss it with my wife."
- "I need to sleep on it."

These objections, and others like them, are heard repeatedly by all salespeople, and have been ever since the first product was marketed. They are clearly excuses—ways of procrastinating—and they are made by individuals who simply haven't been persuaded to make a decision. It is vitally important to note that in most cases the prospect who makes one of these objections is not rejecting you or your product; he is only delaying his decision. The only thing that stands between this objection and the sale is a clear-cut reason why he must act *now.* In other words, you must create urgency.

Regardless of the product you are offering (a piece of real estate, a life insurance policy, industrial equipment), the way to handle any of the above objections is to *emphasize the importance of timing.* As we discussed in Chapter 5, creating urgency is vital in any presentation precisely because so many prospects are procrastinators. The way to counter objections like those mentioned above is to present a convincing explanation of why it is in the prospect's best interest to act today instead of at some time in the future. You must show him how postponing his decision may be costly.

In selling securities, a sense of urgency is natural, since the investment in question may fluctuate in price at any time. A broker should make a point of reminding the prospect of this fact in the presentation. Then, when a procrastinating objection is made, the broker can say, after sympathizing, "I know you agree with me, John, that timing is crucial in anything we do, and more so in dealing with an undervalued issue such as this one." Often no more than this needs to be said, and the salesperson can immediately go into the close.

A life insurance agent can similarly stress the urgency of purchasing a policy immediately. "Your family could be destitute in the event of your untimely death." A real estate agent, by doing his homework and finding out the facts on a property, can use these facts to create a sense of urgency. "The listing on this property has just been renewed, and the price has been reduced. There are two other interested parties. I suggest that you submit a contract at $250,000, before one of them comes in with an offer. You may be able to pick it up for that, and if so, it's a real bargain." In all these cases, the salesperson shows the prospect the urgency of acting *now!*

• "I only buy real estate [municipal bonds, Brand X, etc.]."

Often a prospect will listen to a presentation with some interest, only to object, "Sounds good, but I don't invest in the stock market. I only buy real estate." In another field, he may inform you he only uses Brand X, and that's the way he's always done it. In a sense, he is telling you that he has a preconception that the way he's been doing things is the right way. In answering this objection, you have to stress the unique features and value of what you are offering.

For example, when a prospect objects that he invests only in real estate, a stockbroker might reply, "John, I fully understand what you are saying. And I have observed by the questions you've asked that you are very astute in the way you conduct your business affairs. Therefore, I assume that *what you are primarily interested in is value.*" This key line may be used in relation to *any* product when such an objection is made.

A broker might continue: "Although you have concentrated on investing in real estate, I know you're open-minded enough to recognize that opportunities have occurred in other arenas. I trust that if you owned a property on which large reserves of natural gas and oil were discovered, you would not be dissatisfied. Is that correct?" Here the prospect is drawn into the conversation to express agreement in preparation for the close.

The answer to the objection might continue like this: "Now I know what you're telling me. You're saying that your prime interest is investing in unrecognized values. You like to buy a situation you can acquire at a price that makes sense to you. Isn't that correct?

"Fine, John. That is the reason I called. I have an idea that I'd like to share with you."

In this example, *the salesperson emphasized what the prospect really wanted—value.* He took the objection seriously, but he reminded the prospect that his real interest was in value. And the salesperson then went on to explain the value of what he was offering. This is an effective way to counter that kind of objection, because value is really what determines the desirability of any product or service.

• "I have a friend in the business."

This common objection stymies many salespersons. The friend in the business may even be a relative, and often is. However, that does not mean this is an ironclad and unanswerable objection. In analyzing this objection, you must ask yourself, "Is the prospect interested in giving his business to his friends? Or is he interested in the best opportunity?" Your product may fit his needs better than what his friend is offering. It is a safe bet that the prospect has other interests besides pleasing his friend.

With this thought in mind, an effective response is "Harry, I understand how you feel toward your friend. However, I am sure you would agree with me that *no one has a monopoly on ideas.*" This is an appropriate point to wait for a response.

How you contnue depends, of course, on your field. But if you have a philosophy about your product or service, you will have no difficulty responding. A stockbroker's answer serves as a good model: "What I am primarily interested in is working with you when interesting opportunities develop—ideas we understand and are watching closely—*situations that your other sources aren't always aware of.* After all, both your friend and I have the same objective—to help build your capital." The phrase in italics is important in terms of this response. Note that in no way does the answer put down the prospect's present source. But the phrase does suggest very clearly that *a new source will have something different to offer.* This is a reasonable answer, and the prospect will often agree to give part of his business to the new source on that basis.

• "I can't afford it."

Every salesperson hears the typical money excuses: "I can't afford it. I'm insurance poor already." "All my capital is tied up right now." But if you have done an effective job of screening and qualifying your prospects, then in the majority of cases the prospect *does* have the money; you simply haven't convinced him yet. So the first line of response should be to present additional reasons for buying, in the event that the money objection is basically an excuse.

If the individual protests again that he can't afford to make the transaction, you might say, "I always find that an individual such as yourself has some special funds put away for that very important and unusual situation." Then continue to highlight major selling points and repeat your request for the order.

It is possible that the prospect's funds for the purchase really are limited. If you find additional buying reasons are not generating a response, it may be time to move into "the compromise close." In this close, which is treated fully in Chapter 7, you offer a smaller transaction that may fit his financial situation better.

CONCLUSION

Whether or not you like to deal with objections, you might as well get used to them if you plan to build a career as a salesperson. Objections will always be an integral part of selling in every industry, and it is important to understand how to use them to your advantage. Learn to accept them as requests for additional information. Learn to interpret them to mean "I want your product. Give me a more compelling reason to buy. Convince me!"

It is not always possible to differentiate between real objections and false ones; but then, quite often the prospect doesn't know whether his objection is real, either. The most important thing to remember is that an objection means the prospect is not yet convinced enough to make a buying decision. Therefore, you must continue selling, often answering an objection and closing the sale several times in the course of a single presentation. Remember, too, that the salesperson who asks for the order three times will be dramatically more successful than the individual who asks for the order only once.

To handle every objection ever made, you don't have to memorize a long list of rebuttals. A handful of strong all-purpose answers is more than sufficient when you know how to analyze what the prospect is really saying. Naturally, this requires skill and sensitivity; but remember, top salespersons are made, not born. Once you know what the prospect is really saying, you can select the most effective line of response, and follow it with another request for the order, or, perhaps, the compromise close.

Always remember to answer every objection, even those which may seem unworthy of a reply, in a delicate and understanding way. Above all, never shy away from objections. Accept them as challenges, and meet them head-on. Remind yourself that the sale doesn't begin till the customer says no!

7.

Closing the Sale

This chapter is intended primarily for those salespersons who make daily transactions on the telephone. Some individuals use the telephone only to set up an appointment, and prefer to give the presentation face to face; but whether you close a sale in person or on the telephone, the techniques employed are similar. So even if you don't attempt to create transactions on the telephone, read on. You can still learn about closing the sale.

The salesperson who is accustomed to giving presentations in person is sometimes rather disoriented when he first begins selling by telephone. He may be used to observing visual buying signals, such as nods and facial expressions. He may also have a repertoire of techniques that can't be used over the telephone, such as holding out a pen and saying, "Here, take this and sign where the X is, John. And press hard, there are three copies." He is probably used to picking up a deposit then and there when the sale is closed, which obviously cannot be done on the telephone.

We don't deny that some advantages are real, but that doesn't mean that there are not effective techniques for producing outstanding results over the telephone. And remember, the telephone offers an invaluable benefit: time to make many more presentations. With a higher number of presentations you can close a lower percentage of prospects and still end up with greater volume. As we've said before, selling is a numbers game: *so many calls equal so many presentations equal so many transactions.*

A word of caution: The numbers won't work if your presentation and close are not effective. A professional salesperson who does his homework will close a much higher percentage of sales than a novice does. There's no magic to it. He's just using tested closing techniques that bring home the bacon.

THE MAJOR/MINOR CLOSE

It's a fact that most people don't like to make major decisions. They tend to procrastinate because there's always a risk of making a mistake. And when the decision involves money, an error in judgment can be a painful experience. Minor decisions, on the other hand, are easy to make; few people have difficulty making up their minds about things that are relatively insignificant. The major/minor close takes advantage of this fact. With this technique, the salesperson leads the buyer to make several small decisions, and the sum of these small decisions equals one major decision. In person or on the telephone, the major/minor close is almost always effective.

A travel agent, for instance, may book an expensive vacation by telephone calls. It would obviously be poor selling to ask the prospect, "Are you willing to spend eight thousand dollars for a trip out West?" That's equivalent to saying, "Boy, this is going to cost you an arm and a leg!" It means you're confronting the buyer with a major decision, and more than likely his first reaction will be to say that he has to think it over.

A more effective technique is to close this sale by presenting a series of minor decisions. "Do you want to leave on July second or July ninth?" This gives the prospect a simple choice which he can make by consulting his calendar.

"Well, I guess July ninth would be better."

"And do you prefer a morning or an afternoon flight?"

"Morning. That way we pick up an extra day of vacation."

"Would you rather leave from Kennedy or Newark?"

"Newark is more convenient."

"Tourist or first class?"

"Tourist."

"When you get to Los Angeles, would you prefer to rent a

station wagon or a large sedan? The wagon is a hundred dollars more for the full month."

As you can see, the customer is making a series of small, easy decisions, which amount to a commitment to the trip. By the time the travel agent completes his questioning, the customer has in effect made the major decision. But notice how easy the travel agent made it for him.

ASSUMING THE SALE

A closely related technique, which is also effective on the telephone, is assuming the sale. The salesperson who uses this technique does not present the prospect with questions, but rather makes statements that *assume* a positive answer. For instance, the travel agent in the preceding example might say, "I'm going to see if there's a good excursion package for your family. If so, it will represent a big savings. But whatever I order, I'll get you the lowest possible airfare." Here the agent does not ask the customer if he wants the lowest rate; he assumes it. But more important, the travel agent is talking positively. He did not say, "If you decide to go." He is talking *as if the decision had already been made.* Likewise, he might continue, "I know you'll want to take the family to Disneyland, so I am booking you for one night in a Holiday Inn in Anaheim." Not "Should I book you?" but "I *am* booking you." Finally, the close might be assumed when the travel agent says, "I'll include an invoice with your itinerary, Joe. You should have that by Friday."

Now, notice that the salesperson never actually asked for the order. He never even asked for a decision of any kind. He simply assumed that of course his customer was agreeable. And the customer's consent constituted an affirmative reply. Since the customer didn't say, "No, I don't want that," he was, in effect, saying, "That sounds fine."

Whatever your product or service, you can make statements that assume the sale. "Give me your address, and I'll have it shipped to your attention." "I need two credit references, Walt." "Now I

have to complete an application. How do you spell your last name?"
"Just make out your check to Midwest National in the amount
of . . ."

Many sales are closed with a combination of the two techniques
we have presented so far. A minor question is asked: "Do you prefer
the red or the blue?" Then it is followed by an assumption: "I'll
put you down for three dozen." Throughout the entire closing, a
number of questions and assumptions like this can be made. Always
remember that your purpose in doing this is to allow the prospect
to buy with ease. He is not subjected to the painful task of making
a major decision. These techniques can be applied in practically
every sales situation with every type of prospect. And in every field
they will be effective in closing the sale.

GETTING AGREEMENT

Still another similar technique is that of conditioning the prospect
to say yes. This technique, which was mentioned in the chapter on
overcoming objections, is similar to an old face-to-face technique
in which the salesperson asks a question while nodding affirma-
tively. The theory is that a prospect will have a tendency to mimic
that motion, and it is difficult to say no while nodding yes. In the
same way, the prospect who has become accustomed to saying yes
to you will find it difficult to say no when it's time to close the sale.

You create the habit of agreement essentially by making statements that are so logical and obvious that the prospect has to agree.
You ask for that agreement by saying, "Well, Tom, I think you
would agree with me that . . ." or by making the statement and
then saying, "Would you agree with that?" In addition to getting
the prospect in the habit of saying yes, this method helps to create
rapport between the two of you. You are people who agree with
each other.

SUGGESTING URGENCY

As the chapter on the presentation stressed, a well-planned presentation creates a sense of urgency. If the prospect fails to act *now,*

he will risk a loss of some sort. When the time comes for the close, the urgency must be stressed again. Otherwise, the prospect won't feel the need for making a decision now. While he procrastinates and thinks about it, he is likely to cool off. Always keep in mind that the more time elapses after the presentation, the less likely it is that a sale will be made. As a salesperson, you must strive to have the prospect make the buying decision immediately after the presentation. If he doesn't, the more time passes, the more he will forget the benefits of your product and think about not spending his money.

Observe leading salespersons and you will discover that they always build a suggestion of urgency into the close. A real estate agent may say, "If you don't put in a bid on this home today, Bill, I'm afraid we're going to miss out on it. Two other families have their eyes on it. One couple has seen it twice now." An automobile salesman will say, "This is the last one of this model we have in stock. And with the new models coming out next month, we won't be getting any more. You're not going to be able to get it if you don't buy now. Now, let me work out a special price for you."

A life insurance agent will suggest urgency by telling the prospect, "Harvey, quite frankly, I'm urging you to make application for this policy and let me schedule you for your physical examination immediately. For goodness' sake, your family needs this coverage. And at your age, your health may be good today, but tomorrow could be too late." Almost any salesperson can honestly say these days, "Al, we've been expecting a price increase any day now. But if we put in your order today, we'll guarantee you today's price, even though the price is apt to go up between today and the time of delivery."

A stockbroker might say, "I'm calling you, Frank, because I believe that the time to make this investment is *now.* It's important that we accumulate these shares at twenty or less. At this price the shares are selling below five times earnings. That's extraordinary for a company with such an outstanding record. Let's take advantage of this opportunity. What I suggest is that we accumulate five thousand shares at twenty or less." The broker should then give his client several seconds to respond, and add, "Do you feel comfortable with that?" Without being domineering, the broker has stressed the urgency of making the transaction *now*.

ASKING FOR THE ORDER—AGAIN AND AGAIN

It's amazing how many salespersons try to keep it a secret that they want the prospect's business. They hesitate to ask for the order, and when it's time to close the sale, they blow it! The first thing to remember is Don't be bashful. Close the sale. And if at first you don't succeed, give him some more reasons to buy—and close and close again. Don't be shy about closing several times. Top salespersons concur that most of their sales result from making more than one request for the order. It means they're getting the sales that the average salesperson gives up on!

We have stressed requesting the order early in the presentation. Again, make sure your first request for the order occurs within five minutes or so. Since you have set the stage for your call with a previous call and a letter, your introduction is brief, and you can go immediately into buying reasons without wasting the prospect's valuable time. By doing this you have a great advantage over telephone salespersons who give their presentations "cold," in the first conversation with the prospect. Use the extra time you have gained to answer objections and ask for the order—again and again.

Each time you request the order and your prospect objects, you should say something like "Fine. I can understand that." Always show understanding. You can then give him an additional reason why he should make the transaction now. Get him back on what is called "the road to commitment" by asking for his agreement, perhaps on the urgency: "You agree with me that timing is critical?" After you have gained agreement, ask for the order again.

Bob Kennedy, now a development officer at Ohio State University, confirms that he routinely asked for the order several times during each call when soliciting funds over the telephone while he was director of development at Capital University (also in Columbus, Ohio). Prior to making a telephone call, Bob would review an individual's background to determine his capacity to make a contribution. In this way, he came up with a fixed amount of money to request from each individual.

"I think it's imperative," Bob states, "no matter what a person is selling, that he knows in advance how big an 'order' to ask for. So very early in the conversation, I'd suggest an amount, say a thousand dollars. If the individual felt that amount was too high, he'd let me know later in the conversation. Many people did this by asking, 'Well, how much do you think *I* should give?'

"This was often a hint that I should come up with a lower figure, so I'd say, 'John, last year you gave six hundred, and with the tremendous need right now, coupled with inflation, would you consider giving eight hundred this year?' I might add that the word 'consider' is a key word—it's very soft sell."

Bob also made a policy of asking for a high amount, knowing that he could come down. "You'd be surprised," he explains, "how many people are flattered that you thought they could afford a big contribution; they don't want to let you down. Of course, if my predetermined amount was too high, I would keep right on asking until a figure was agreed upon."

Bob stresses that asking for the order again and again—even though he used a soft sell—was vital to his success. "The important thing is to *ask* for the money," he emphasizes, "and don't be bashful about asking more than once if you don't get it the first time!"

OFFERING ALTERNATIVES

As Bob Kennedy's success demonstrates, there are times when you should recognize the need for a *compromise*, particularly if you have not convinced the prospect by the third request. Maybe he's saying, "I'll have to check my funds." Of course you're aware that by this he might mean "I am not convinced. I don't see the urgency. Your story isn't conclusive." But he may also be making a valid objection; he cannot, for some reason, make a transaction of this size right now. In this case, you can offer a psychological compromise by using the maxi-mini, or compromise, close. In this close you state that your original suggestion may be the desirable maximum transaction, but that a smaller transaction may be appropriate at this time.

For instance, a stockbroker who has suggested an initial purchase of five thousand shares may now say, "John, I can understand by what you have told me that you are not prepared at this time to take a full position. But you do agree with me that this investment can benefit you substantially. Furthermore, in anything we do together, timing is a primary consideration. So what I'd like to do is simply this. Let's not make that maximum investment now which you would make had you the funds available at this time. Instead, let's take advantage of the timing of this investment and at least make a minimum commitment. I suggest three thousand shares."

At this point, a long pause is in order. If the prospect hesitates and is still uncertain, you can add, "Or would you feel more comfortable with two thousand shares?"

The compromise close is a useful response to money excuses no matter what you sell. A life insurance agent can use a version of the preceding response. "George, I can understand from what you've said that you are not prepared at this time to invest in a $200,000 policy. But you do agree with me that insurance is important, and that it's one purchase that cannot wait. So what I'd like to do is this. Let's not make that maximum investment you would make if you had the funds available. Instead, let's make a minimum commitment that will at least guarantee some security for the present. Do you feel comfortable with $100,000?"

It is easy to tailor this response in the same way to any product. Every salesperson can use the compromise close in response to money objections. "Do you feel comfortable with fifty gross at this time?" And, after a pause, "Or would you prefer to purchase forty gross?" "Do you feel comfortable with a full page to start off your advertising program, or would you prefer to go with the half page at this time?"

With the compromise close, you're working on the premise that half a loaf is better than no bread. Every salesperson can find a way to offer an uncomfortable prospect an alternative. The real estate agent who is attempting to obtain a listing, for instance, should have in mind the price range he thinks is legitimate for a specific house. The homeowner, however, is sometimes uncomfortable with the suggested asking price. Knowing this, an agent can begin the close by saying to the homeowner, "Fred, after doing a careful market analysis of your home, I suggest an asking price of $180,-000. Do you feel comfortable with that?" If the homeowner makes it clear that he does not, the agent can add, "Fine. What price would you feel comfortable with?" This question opens the way for discussion and compromise.

THE WRAP-UP

When a telephone sale is concluded, summarize the order and express your thanks for the business. "Herb, I'm going to run over this order now to make sure I've got it straight. That's model 411. Quantity: four dozen small, ten dozen medium, and eight dozen large. Assorted colors. That's twenty-two dozen at $90 per dozen, for a total of $1,980. We will ship them F.O.B. New York tomorrow, and the invoice will follow. I'll give you a call later this month to see how they're moving, okay? . . . Thanks again for your business, Herb. I really appreciate it."

The wrap-up is more important on the telephone than in face-to-face selling, because only a verbal agreement has been made. The customer did not sign an order blank; there is nothing to verify the transaction. For this reason, you should always forward a letter to the customer to confirm the order and prevent misunderstandings. In some cases, a follow-up telephone call is also appropriate, and will eliminate errors in communication. Your assistant, if you have one, can make these confirming calls to free up selling time for you. "Mr. Zimmer, I'm Carol Dey, Ted Green's assistant, and I have just a few quick questions to go over with you regarding your order."

CONCLUSION

Closing a sale on the telephone is different in some respects from closing in person, but the results can be every bit as good. In fact, when you consider how many more presentations you can give by using the phone, you have the opportunity to make many more sales. There are several effective techniques for closing on the telephone, and they will work regardless of what you sell.

The most important thing to remember is Don't keep it a secret why you're calling. Request the order—and do it again and again. There's no law against attempting to close a number of times. The closing is the moment of truth. Unless you get a commitment from your prospect, you haven't really been selling. *Nothing happens until the sale is closed.*

8

Follow-Up

In the world of business it is frequently said that "nothing happens till something is sold." For the telephone salesperson, this statement might be revised to read, "Nothing happens until the sale is followed up." If a salesperson does not follow up a verbal telephone transaction, he will never develop his accounts into substantial clients. *Sales minus follow-up equals lost production.*

The term "follow-up" can mean different things to different people. Basically it refers to events that occur after the sale is made. Follow-up begins when the transaction has been completed, and continues for the entire lifetime of your relationship with the client. Good follow-up means doing what you say you're going to do. It means doing what you're expected to do—and more. Good follow-up gives you credibility and places you head and shoulders above the army of salespersons who also want your client's business.

This sounds basic, and it is. Yet the majority of salespersons pay little attention to follow-up, and as a result their earnings are substantially reduced. Stop and reflect: How many times have you received a letter thanking you for your business after you purchased an expensive automobile? A life insurance policy? A thousand shares of stock? A new home? A piece of office equipment? And how often have you been disappointed by salespeople who didn't follow up? Think back on your frustration in dealing with those people. Remember the order that came in three weeks late, but you never received a call from the salesperson explaining why? Do you recall how you felt about the salesperson who said he would mail you some papers or drop off some brochures, but never got around to it? Unfortunately, we have all had enough experiences like this to make us realize that the salesperson who performs *after* the sale is worth his weight in gold.

WHEN DOES FOLLOW-UP BEGIN?

The follow-up process can't begin too soon. In fact, in telephone selling it starts the moment the sale is closed—*before* you put down the receiver. Too many salespersons are overly eager to hang up as soon as a transaction occurs. They react as though the buyer may change his mind if they stay on the line. So they give him the rush act: "Okay, I'll put you down for two thousand units at twenty dollars each. Thanks a lot, Harry, good-bye."

These same salespersons are sometimes so anxious to make the next call that they fail to make adequate notes of the transaction. By the end of the day they have forgotten some of the details of the sales they have made. It's no wonder that their customers receive mixed-up orders, with products in the wrong sizes and colors and styles. Even if the order does go through correctly, salespersons such as these seldom have a system for following up to insure that the customer was satisfied, and to build the new customer into an account. Their lack of follow-up results in returned or canceled orders, frustrated customers, and few, if any, reorders.

As we have said, follow-up begins concurrently with the transaction. When the customer places the order, congratulate him and welcome him to your company. Explain any resources your company has to offer him. It's important to realize that you are setting the stage for the next call. In most fields, the first transaction does not mean you've reached your goal. It merely means you've broken the ice with the client. Now is the time to develop a closer relationship. The client made a commitment he feels comfortable about. Now is the time to build.

In opening any new account, certain information must be obtained about the client. Review that information to become better acquainted with the client's background. Then immediately forward a letter thanking him for his business. The letter should reiterate the important details of the transaction.

There may also be enclosures that will help cement the relationship. A broker, for instance, wants the client to become involved with the company he's invested in. So the letter should include an annual report, a quarterly statement, and the brokerage firm's written recommendation on the investment. This material will stimulate the client to become more personally involved. It will also remind him that the broker's firm has made a sophisticated in-depth analysis before asking him to participate.

Immediately following the conversation with a new account, a salesperson should make a note on the 3×5 card he has kept on the client since the first call, marking down all information concerning the transaction, as well as his impression of the individual and the conversation. If the client was excited about the purchase, that should be noted. Perhaps he said that within the next few weeks he would have some cash coming in and could conceivably make a larger purchase. The salesperson should note that, too.

Then, and this is a very significant part of follow-up, the date of the next call should be noted. The card should be placed in a chronological follow-up file to be sure the call is placed at the appropriate time. This kind of detail work is an appropriate way to follow up an order in any field.

GOODWILL CALLS

With a 1980 production of nearly $7 million, Stan Glick is considered one of America's top salespersons in the field of upholstered furniture. Stan represents International Furniture and Karpen Furniture in a wide territory that covers Kentucky, Indiana, and southern Ohio. "This is a very personalized business," he explains. "Typically, a salesperson will make an in-person call on his customers every couple of weeks just to make sure everything is going smoothly. But my territory is too big for me to do that, so I use

the phone, especially to contact customers in out-of-the-way areas."
These are goodwill calls, but Stan often finds that they also generate additional business. "I'll call and say, 'What's going on?' " he
explains, "or I'll ask, 'What's moving?' If the company has recently
shipped out a new style, I'll ask, 'How's number so-and-so moving?
Oh, really? That's great! You'll be wanting some more shipped out
then.'

"Like I said, these calls not only create goodwill, but they also
generate sales. And they build up customer loyalty, which is so
important in a highly competitive field like mine."

As Stan implies, goodwill built through follow-up calls is a vitally
important *preventive;* it keeps business that might otherwise be lost
to a more aggressive competitor. Before problems arise and business is lost, it pays to think of what you can do to prevent that from
happening.

Bill Frankenstein, the life insurance agent previously mentioned,
routinely calls every client a day or two after the policy is purchased. "There's a tendency for 'buyer's remorse' to set in with life
insurance," Bill explains. "Because it's an intangible, some people
begin to cool off and regret their decision. It used to be a serious
problem. I was losing 15 to 20 percent of my sales—they'd just cool
off and decide they wanted to do something else with their
money."

Now, very soon after Bill submits the application to the company, he makes a goodwill call to the client. "I'll say something like
'Say, Joe, I just called to congratulate you on your good judgment
in applying for a $200,000 policy. And I wanted to remind you to
call me any time if there's anything at all you need. When your
policy is approved, I'll deliver it to you personally. Again, congratulations on making a wise decision."

Bill explains that since he began making these follow-up calls, he
has rarely lost a sale due to buyer's remorse. "Another thing," he
adds, "it's remarkable how grateful they are for the call. They'll say,
'I've never had a salesman call me *after* the sale.' And when I've
bought something like a car or a home, or made an investment, I

too would appreciate a call like that. What amazes me is that this kind of follow-up call isn't taught by every sales organization. In fact, sales managers should require it! It's such a little thing, and the results are fantastic."

While goodwill calls often lead directly to further sales, it is sometimes important to refrain from discussing business during these calls. Experienced salespersons point out that some clients simply need a lot of "stroking." Above all, these clients do not want to see dollar signs in the salesperson's eyes. "You've got to show the client you *care* about him as an individual," one successful stockbroker says. "Every day I make a certain number of goodwill calls in which I purposely avoid discussing the market. I might call just to say hello, or I might want to arrange a golf game or congratulate a client on his son's graduation from college." Professional salespersons like this one are adept at understanding human nature and unanimously agree that "everyone likes to be stroked." A non-business call to a client helps build a lasting relationship.

A word of caution, however: Not everybody has time for small talk. You must know your client. What is a pleasant little chat to one person is an annoying interruption to another. Exercise judgment, or a friendly call can do more harm than good.

Joe Girard, listed in *The Guiness Book of World Records* as Greatest Salesman, holds the all-time record for automobile sales: 1,425 individual units sold in 1973. Joe believes that his use of the telephone to create goodwill has been a major factor in his success. Since early in his career, he has used the telephone during slow times to call everybody he could think of that might one day buy a car. "And that," he points out, "is practically everybody.

"I'll call an old customer and say, 'Where in the world have you been?' He'd reply, 'Er, Joe, I haven't needed a car recently.' I'd say, 'Do you have to need a car to stop in and say hello? I know you go right by here on the way to work. I want you to stop in and say hello. Now, tell me about yourself. How you doing?'

"It's simply a matter of showing people that you care for them," Joe points out. "When I sell a car, my customer knows I care. That feeling can be conveyed over the phone, too. If I call a guy just to say hello, he knows I didn't forget him the minute the sale was made."

Joe emphasizes that goodwill can snowball. "It's like when you walk out of a restaurant," he says, "and you say to your wife, 'Honey, remind me never to go back in there again, will ya?' Do you know what builds great restaurants? Word of mouth. Because people tell other people how much they *care* for you in that restaurant. The great restaurants in this country have love and care coming out of their kitchens, and their reputations are built on that." The same principle applies to salespersons who care about their customers.

Every retail salesperson can learn a lesson from Joe Girard. During the course of a day there are usually slow periods when a salesperson can use his time most productively by making goodwill calls to customers.

Many aggressive retail salespeople also create goodwill by calling "special" customers now and then. One saleswoman who owns a woman's clothing boutique does exactly that. She may call one customer to say, "Helen, you've got to come in today. I just got in a perfect dress in your size." Or just before a big sale, she may call to say, "Jeanne, our fall sale starts tomorrow, and you won't believe the bargains! Now, if you want me to, I'll pull out a few things in your size and hold them. But you'll have to be sure to come in first thing in the morning, okay?" There's no question about it—customers feel good about a call like this which gives them special attention.

TENDING TO THE DETAILS

Doing necessary detail work is paramount in successful follow-up. While every customer expects a salesperson to take care of the important matters, it is a rare individual who follows up on the little details. Yet this extra effort above and beyond the call of duty is precisely what generates customer respect and loyalty. Without exception, leading salespersons treat every detail as important. By tending to follow-up promptly, they never get buried in a mass of paperwork. Detail is an integral part of their working day. The reason is simple. They know that what seems like a minor detail to them may be of prime concern to the customer!

A professional stockbroker does not forget the customer after the follow-up thank-you letter. His chronological file will remind him to send out updated research on the investment. He will also forward news clippings that might be of interest. If there is some especially pertinent information, he will personally call the customer to fill him in. Follow-up means taking care of the details in an ongoing way. While no single piece of information may be vital, the accumulated follow-up is highly impressive.

This kind of attention is necessary in any field. A good life insurance agent, for instance, will find numerous occasions for follow-up phone calls. After the transaction is agreed upon, he will call the client to make sure there are no complications in scheduling the physical examination. He may call at a later time to ask whether the client's attorney and CPA have been advised of the proposed policy in order to coordinate it with his estate planning and tax planning. The agent will also offer to review the proposed policy with them and perhaps also with the client's spouse. Later, when the policy is issued, he will be sure to call the client to congratulate him and to set up a time to deliver the policy in person.

The agent who gives this kind of attention to detail is going to be well received when he periodically calls with an offer to review the client's complete insurance program. Sure, he could have left the scheduling of the physical exam to chance, and mailed the policy with a brief note, or no letter at all. But the time devoted to follow-up has demonstrated to the client that the agent *cares* and can be trusted to do a thorough job. The follow-up makes him a true professional in his field. The salesperson who doesn't follow up may be an authority in his product but he is not likely to get referrals and repeat business!

Regardless of your field, every detail must be tended to, and the telephone is usually the quickest way to accomplish this. But a good salesperson should be creative. The best follow-up often coordinates telephone calls with mail, and sometimes in-person visits. Whatever combination of methods works best for you, be sure to take care of the details, and to let the customer know about them.

KEEPING THE CUSTOMER INFORMED

A stockbroker who is interested in building goodwill with a client will find a wealth of reasons to make a telephone call. A client might be called, for instance, when a company in his portfolio has declared a higher dividend. Another call might serve to explain why a company's quarterly earnings are down. Perhaps a change in management explains a stock's fluctuations. Whatever the reason for the call, the broker is letting the client know that he *cares;* he is closely watching his client's portfolio. He is in business not just to sell but also to inform. The client who receives these calls realizes that "this broker is different. He's interested in my welfare; he's a professional."

To cite another example, a real estate agent also has many occasions for calls: a VA appraisal may be scheduled; perhaps the comments of a prospective buyer should be passed on; the wording of an ad for the newspaper might be checked. In general, a homeowner is not aware of one-tenth of what an agent does on his behalf —and that's because the agent doesn't inform him! Unfortunately, good communication is an exception to the rule. The salesperson who does maintain contact with his accounts will stand out far above the crowd. And over a period of time, he will gain his clients' loyalty.

COMMUNICATING BAD NEWS

As every salesperson knows, there are times when unpleasant information must be communicated to the customer. An insurance agent may want to put off calling a client when a life policy has been heavily rated by the company (meaning that his policy will require a higher premium than quoted). The agent knows this is bad news, and the customer will be unhappy, but the longer the agent waits, the more upset the customer is likely to become. A real estate agent does not enjoy calling a potential buyer to let him know that someone else made a better offer, or telling a homeowner that the couple he just showed the house to are not interested. An automobile salesperson will not relish calling a person who was a difficult sale in the first place to tell him that there will be a two-week delay in delivery. An advertising salesperson may put off a call notifying a client that it was impossible to place the ad in a particular publication because he has not made the deadline.

In these and countless other cases, salespersons naturally shy away from communicating bad news. Yet follow-up is never more important than when a problem exists. Most problems can be resolved, and most customer dissatisfaction can be nipped in the bud, if you communicate. Regardless of the problem, it is necessary to follow up.

No matter how thoroughly you do your part, there will inevitably be awkward situations from time to time. Putting off difficult telephone calls only compounds the problem. Most of the time, if you face the music, the difficulty can be resolved. In fact, more serious problems result from procrastination than from anything else.

Every stockbroker will agree that it's a pleasure to call a client and discuss his good fortune in making an investment that has gone up in value. But the typical broker does not communicate with his clients regarding an investment that has declined in price. No matter how thorough an analysis may be, every stockbroker will have a certain number of disappointed clients. But most will avoid contacting these investors, and this is a serious mistake.

A stockbroker-client relationship is built over a period of time. When an investment declines, the key is to get back to the client and talk to him about the basics of the company. Are they changed or unchanged? Many times an analysis shows that the company remains an excellent investment despite a decline in price. When that is the case, a good broker will say something like this to the client: "John, we purchased five thousand shares of Great American Oil ten days ago at twenty-five. It's now twenty-two. But the first and most important consideration relates to the company itself. Our review shows that there has been no change in the basics of the company. As you and I discussed, this investment was made to achieve long-term capital gains, so the investment will be held on to for a minimum period of twelve to eighteen months. At the present price, we're all the more enthusiastic about Great American, and I suggest that we increase our investment." By making this call and suggesting further investment, the broker reinforces his client's confidence in both himself *and* the investment.

The majority of clients don't give up on a salesperson because of some problem with the transaction. Instead, they leave a salesperson who fails to keep them informed. Clients need an opportunity to communicate, particularly when there's been a disappointment. Generally, the people who are most successful in sales are the ones who are willing to make the difficult calls other people avoid.

CREATING CREDIBILITY

To firmly establish a new account, you must create an image of credibility in your customer's mind. You are a person he can depend on. In most cases, your client is in a position to choose the salesperson he wants to do business with. Your competitors are willing and eager for his account, and, always remember, your client can more than likely buy the same product from one of them. Therefore, he will deal with the salesperson who establishes credibility.

No matter how convincing your presentation, or how quickly a friendly relationship has been established with the new customer, he may still have a certain amount of doubt. "Have I been sold a bill of goods? Is this guy really as good as he says he is?" The customer has almost certainly had disappointments in the past.

Unless you follow up after the sale, you will jeopardize the transaction and risk losing his future business as well.

Imagine how delighted a doubting Thomas is when continuing follow-up demonstrates to him that you *do* perform. Think how impressed he is when he receives follow-up material immediately after the telephone transaction. Attractive material and a personal letter, promptly mailed, tell him that you're a person he can rely on. The degree of professionalism in your follow-up is the final touch that establishes your credibility.

THE PERSONAL TOUCH

An added touch, often overlooked, is follow-up that involves your client personally. This can be as simple as a telephone call at your client's home congratulating him on a special event. Of course, this added personal touch is not really necessary, but once again, it's the extra effort that makes a salesperson shine.

As you build a relationship with a client, you may discover his special interest or hobby. He might collect stamps or coins or art. Many people are devoted to some particular sport, for instance, golf, jogging, or tennis. Whatever a client's avocation, if you come across a book or article about it that you think he might enjoy, by all means, mail it to him. You may read an article which relates to his business or industry; if so, be sure to forward it to him. This kind of follow-up shows your client that you see him as more than an account; you're interested in his general success and well-being.

Many service-oriented industries lend themselves naturally to the personal touch. An insurance agent, for instance, has files which show his clients' birthdates, so he can easily send out birthday cards or, better yet, call to wish the person a happy birthday. Similarly, a real estate agent can bring a house gift, such as a plant or an attractive nameplate for the front door, to a new homeowner. A personal touch does not have to be expensive or showy. It's enough that you took the time to do it.

Diana Bloch, a successful travel agent in Columbus, Ohio, relies heavily on the telephone to sell her services. Since, as she points out, the travel accommodations she offers can also be purchased through her competition, she believes in adding her own personal touch. "If a couple are celebrating a special anniversary," she explains, "I'll tip off the hotel. Or if they're going on a cruise, I have a special bottle of wine or champagne delivered to their cabin. And, since my husband and I have done quite a bit of traveling ourselves, I can often send a list of good restaurants to clients who are visiting a city for the first time. Of course, I follow up with the standard brochures and information and itineraries. But I find that the added personal touch is what builds customer loyalty."

BUILDING A CLIENTELE THROUGH FOLLOW-UP

When discussing follow-up, it's important to note that although you have made an initial transaction, you still do not have a client —only an account. An account does not become a client, a steadfast customer, until repeated transactions have built a lasting relationship. The vital ingredient that turns accounts into clients is professional follow-up.

In almost every industry, approximately 20 percent of your clients account for about 80 percent of your total sales. By concentrating on building existing accounts into clients, you can discover that vital 20 percent. Too often, a salesperson will make a strong effort to open a new account—only to desert the customer once the business is on the books! What such a salesperson fails to see is that he is only scratching the surface of the business he could obtain.

Experienced salespeople know that a small order can develop into a significant account over a period of time. Turning that account into a client often requires only minor attention to the details of follow-up, certainly less effort than going through the entire process of prospecting and making the necessary presentations to acquire a new account. Disorganized salespeople, however, often neglect their follow-up in their eagerness to solicit new prospects. As a result, they never realize the great potential that can be achieved through a solid clientele.

In developing your own follow-up system, it's helpful to picture a satisfied client not as a one-time transaction but as a *profit center*. That client potentially represents X amount of business each and every year. Moreover, he is your base for future referrals. In a sense, a new client is like a gold mine. You can either be satisfied with taking small nuggets off the surface, or you can decide the mine should be thoroughly worked and developed. The resource is there, but only follow-up will develop the full potential. The failure to mine this valuable resource is probably the greatest waste of time and effort there is in telephone selling. Always remember, you're in business not just to open new accounts but to build and develop a clientele.

Bob Burnett, a leading sales counselor for an employment agency in Lima, Ohio, is a good illustration of how to build a clientele through follow-up. "I follow up on every placement I make," Bob explains. "I call both parties, the employer and the employee. It's just a friendly 'How are you?' call to show my clients that I really care about them. For instance, I say, 'Hello, Jack, this is Bob Burnett, and I just called to touch bases with you. How do you like it there? Great! I knew you'd feel right at home with the company.' Then I call the employer to make sure he's satisfied with his new employee. You'd be surprised how many times he'll say something like 'Bob, boy am I glad you called. We've been thinking about putting on some additional help, and you're just the man I want to talk to.' "

The more exposure you have with your customers, the more sales you are going to be exposed to. And, according to so many leading salespersons, a telephone call intended for goodwill often results in additional business.

FOLLOW-UP ON SPECIAL OCCASIONS

Particular occasions may be good openings for follow-up calls. An insurance agent, for instance, can call a client: "Congratulations on your daughter's marriage. I understand it was a beautiful wedding." This may be a good opportunity to add later, "We haven't reviewed your coverage for quite some time. What do you say we get together for lunch next Tuesday?" A real estate agent can also read the newspapers for any news of changes in a client's life. A new baby may mean the house is getting crowded; a son or daughter getting married may mean it's time for a smaller house. In addition, an ambitious agent will have a schedule of daily calls to previous clients, so that each and every one is reached every six months or so. Who knows when a satisfied client might be ready to move up, be transferred, or know somebody else who's in the market for a house?

CONCLUSION

Follow-up begins the instant the sale is closed. In any field, attention to detail is what separates the real professionals from the run-of-the-mill salespeople. And it is just as important to convey bad news promptly as it is to attend to more pleasant calls. While salespeople sometimes perceive follow-up as unproductive time, because it does not seem to lead straight to a transaction, nothing could be further from the truth. Good follow-up, often with a personal touch, builds credibility and develops a solid clientele.

In a highly competitive marketplace, a telephone call is an excellent inexpensive way to show a customer that you care about him. A call to say, "Hello, is there anything I can do?" is an added touch that builds customer loyalty. In business, as anywhere else, thoughtfulness is always appreciated. A friendly call conveys an interest in the customer that goes beyond the business relationship. You want to say hello and to offer help because you're interested in *his* welfare.

Over the long run, attention to detail and conscientious follow-up build successful sales careers. The truth is, follow-up is just as essential in professional telephone selling as prospecting and closing. Sure, it's exciting to open a new account, but a significant client will give you sale after sale, year after year. Every new account is a potential gold mine. You can't afford to ignore it.

9.

Servicing
the Customer

In our highly competitive marketplace, servicing after the telephone sale is paramount. The Red Queen in *Alice in Wonderland* could very well have had servicing a customer in mind when she advised Alice, "Now, here you see, it takes all the running you can do to keep in the same place. If you want to get somewhere else, you must run twice as fast!" A company's very survival in the 1980s may well depend upon its ability to extend service after the sale. Likewise, the modern salesperson must be service-oriented if he is to maintain his hard-earned accounts.

COMMUNICATION—THE NAME OF THE GAME

It's impossible to give good service to a customer if you fail to communicate with him. Sometimes simply calling him to pass along information is viewed as outstanding service in itself. Rich Port, one of the most successful Realtors in America, believes that communication is one of the most important ingredients in successful selling. Quite often, according to Rich, it's important to inform the customer of what you as his salesperson actually do for him. In fact, as Rich points out, the only way the customer *can* know about it is if the salesperson communicates with him. Selling real estate is a good example. A 6 percent commission on a home priced at $150,000 will be $9,000. If the seller doesn't know the behind-the-scenes work involved, he is likely to think the agent didn't earn that commission.

"When you find a frustrated, disgruntled seller," Rich says, "it's because he hasn't been kept informed about what's happening with his home. It's usually just plain bad communication. A client should never, and I repeat, *never,* have to call the agent to find out what's happening. A good professional is constantly in touch with the seller.

"He may call to say, 'We just received a mortgage commitment on your property this morning.' He may call back later and say, 'The buyer who looked at it yesterday probably isn't going to buy, but I have someone coming in tonight. I suggest you keep the lights on in the living room, the ones on the end tables. How's eight P.M.?' He may tell the seller, 'A VA appraiser is coming out on Wednesday around two. Is that all right?'

"If there's nothing to call about," Rich continues, "the agent should find something and let the customer know what he's working on. 'Today we submitted your home to the multiple listing service. Tomorrow a photographer is coming out to take a picture of the home.' Or he might call to say, 'I wrote this ad last night. Before I submit it to the newspapers, I'd like to read it to you.' The secret is to keep in constant touch with the seller. Let him know what's happening. The typical real estate office does much more to merchandise a piece of property than the seller knows. *And that's because no one tells him!* A salesperson can do all these things and keep it a secret, and he'll end up with a frustrated seller."

Many salespersons believe that "the sale doesn't actually happen until *after* the sale has been made." This refers, of course, to the importance of service after the sale. Successful salespeople all share this philosophy. As Rich Port emphasizes, "Service, service, service. You've got to kill your customers with service—*even after they have purchased a home.*" He believes in giving customers so much service that they'll feel guilty about even thinking of going elsewhere with their business.

Two other highly successful real estate agents, identical twins Greg and John Rice of West Palm Beach, Florida, also stress the importance of communicating with clients *after* they purchase a home. "So many people orphan their customers," John says. "They forget that eventually that customer is going to need a new home, and abandon him after the sale has been made. We don't do that. If the home turns out not to have a key to the garage door, for example, that's not the buyer's problem—that's *our* problem."

In the case of leased equipment, such as computers, copying machines, and heavy machinery, the competition is quite strong. Often the product offered by one company is very little different from the products offered by competitors. In the final analysis, it is service that will determine who gets the business. Again, telephone follow-up can be an important factor in keeping the business.

Many representatives of firms that lease equipment desert their customers after the lease is signed, feeling that if anything goes wrong, the problem belongs with the service department. Maintaining the account, however, is the job of the sales representative. When a copy machine, for instance, is installed, a phone call the following week is in order. "Hello, Bill. I just called to see how you're getting along with the new machine. Are the copies good? . . . I'm glad I called, because it's not supposed to do that. I'll put in a service request right now. And I'll check back with you in a few days. In the meantime, don't hesitate to call me."

A call like this can save an account that might have been lost when the lease expired. All too often, representatives fail to realize that leases are not automatically renewed. Frequently the service is provided month to month, and the customer can terminate with a pro rata refund at any time. After the contract is signed, the salesperson should think of the sale as an ongoing activity and never take the customer for granted. If he does, he'll quickly discover that the competition is more than willing to take over.

In many other business relationships, the sale is also ongoing. The insurance industry is a case in point. Most agents assume that once a policy is issued, the sale is over, and the renewal commissions will automatically roll in without any future servicing. But the professional agent knows better and constantly keeps in touch with his clients to update their coverage.

Alan Weiler, a leading insurance broker in Columbus, Ohio, is a strong believer in servicing his existing clientele. When silver prices rose dramatically in 1979, Alan called his clients to discuss changing their coverage. In a typical call, he would say, "Bob, we've had several claims submitted for stolen silverware during the past few months, and our clients have been shocked to realize how high the replacement cost is now. I was looking at your policy, and I figure the cost of silver has gone up 600 percent since we listed the value of your silverware." Alan found that although his clients were aware of silver increases, they hadn't thought of increasing their homeowner's policies. Every client was grateful for Alan's thoughtfulness, and they all had their policies updated.

Even in many fields which we do not relate to selling, telephone servicing is appropriate at times. Dick Ary, a Columbus CPA, frequently calls his clients to keep them up to date on tax planning. "Do you have a few minutes for some questions?" He then goes on with questions that relate to income, a need for tax shelter investments, whether the client is planning to sell any securities, and so on.

It is not always possible to drop in on a client just to say hello, nor is such a visit always welcome. What Dick accomplishes with his clients in ten minutes on the phone would probably take at least an hour in the office, and neither Dick nor the client has the time. Dick's habit of following up with his clients throughout the year is a factor in the fine reputation he enjoys, and it helps him maintain his clients year after year. And doesn't it just make good business sense for everybody, regardless of the nature of his business or profession, to communicate with the people who represent his bread and butter?

INSTANT CONTACT BY TELEPHONING

Communication involves more than just letting the customer know what you are doing for him. Often there is an urgent need to pass on information to customers, and the telephone may be the only way to do this. A company may have knowledge of upcoming favorable publicity for a product, and have no other way to notify customers in time. A book publisher, for instance, might get a late booking for an author appearing on *The Bob Braun Show*, a television talk show based in Cincinnati which also reaches large markets in Dayton, Columbus, Indianapolis, Lexington, and Louisville. Bookstores in these markets can be called and told about the appearance. The publisher's representative might say, "This talk show always generates many requests for an author's book. I suggest we restock your present inventory so you can meet the demand created by this appearance."

A similar situation occurs in the case of a product which is a response to a particular event. After the NFL playoffs, for instance, merchandise promoting the winning team sells well until the Super Bowl game. This is one of many cases where telephone servicing is far and away the best means of selling the product. *The shortest distance between two points is not a straight line but a telephone call!* A sudden change in the weather creates the same sort of situation; most people, for instance, wait until the snow is knee-deep before they rush out to buy fur-lined boots. Such items as shovels, umbrellas, raincoats, topcoats, gloves, ski equipment, and air conditioning units may be subject to sudden heavy demand. When this happens, quick phone calls to major accounts can generate business which would have been lost if servicing depended on a salesperson making an in-person call.

When a new fad opens up a potential market, telephone servicing is often the best way to capitalize on it. The classic example occurred years ago when Walt Disney's *Davy Crockett* television series zoomed up in the ratings. Watching the show, a St. Louis furrier recognized a tremendous potential for sales of coonskin caps. He also realized that it would take months to man a sales force to visit all his retail accounts. Consequently, he hired ten women and began a coast-to-coast telephone campaign. Within one week, the saleswomen had reached every one of his customers. As a result, he ended up with 85 percent of all coonskin hat business. His willingness to be innovative gave him otherwise impossible results. The point of this example cannot be too heavily stressed: Telephone servicing is not only the least expensive way and the fastest way of selling—it is often the *only* way.

With inflation as it is, many companies find relatively sudden price changes necessary from time to time. Notifying customers in advance of these changes is an excellent use of the telephone. Giving customers a chance to reorder at the old prices is a courtesy they appreciate, and one that helps to soften the impact of a price increase.

THE INCOMING CALL

Telephone service calls can be both outgoing and incoming. While thus far we have confined our discussion to calls instituted by the salesperson, it is also important to encourage the customer to initiate the call, because you might not always call at a time when he is having a problem. In many cases, problems can be solved quickly via the telephone, with no personal visit needed. Thus, not only do you decrease your expenses, but you save your customer time.

At Xerox, Shelby Carter explains, "when one of our machines stops working, a customer will phone Xerox Service. In order to avoid unnecessary service calls, we've tested a program called 'Call Avoidance.' When a customer phones to request service, we talk the customer through a diagnostic check. The customer tests some possible solutions. We are able to solve up to 7 percent of the service problems without having to dispatch a technician. This program has several advantages: first, it immediately gives back to the customer the use of his copying machine; second, it saves Xerox the expense of making a call; and finally, it keeps everyone's costs down. We pass on our productivity savings by holding the price line against inflation. In the long run, the customer wins."

Shelby continues: "At first we were skeptical of customer reaction. Would a customer be willing to spend fifteen to twenty minutes with us on the phone to try to fix the machine himself? Early tests show customers are willing to participate; they see the advantages and will take the time."

Today, companies all over the country are encouraging their local customers to call whenever a problem arises. "We're as close as your local phone" is a common slogan.

According to sales executives who have set up successful programs, three important rules of handling all incoming service calls are:

1. **Make the customer feel comfortable in calling.** It should go without saying that the receptionist who is the first to speak with the caller must extend a warm greeting. The representatives who handle the incoming calls must be friendly and courteous.

2. **Handle the call smoothly and efficiently.** Everyone who may answer an incoming call for service must know who can take care of the problem. "For heaven's sake," says one service manager, "make sure the customer isn't given the runaround and transferred from department to department." Servicing by telephone can't be haphazard—it's got to be an organized effort.

3. **Don't keep the customer waiting.** If the sales representative is not available, or it is impossible to give an immediate explanation, don't put the customer on hold. Instead, take his name and number and have the proper person call him back—again, as quickly as possible.

WATS LINES

While there is no difficulty in getting local customers to call you, dissatisfied out-of-town customers usually resent long-distance charges. Even when they are encouraged to call collect, they sometimes feel awkward about having a stranger accept the charges and, in fact, are not really confident the charges will be accepted. A toll-free service can be the ideal solution to servicing out-of-town customers. Of course, a small company may not be able to afford an incoming WATS (Wide Area Telephone Service) line. But bear in mind that a WATS line doesn't have to be national. By checking with your local telephone company, you can find out whether a smaller area (where you service your customers) might be more appropriate. The telephone company will also assist you by surveying your most recent long-distance calls to see if a WATS line is feasible for you.

In considering a WATS line, you must weigh the anticipated cost against the expected increase in business. This added service can sometimes give you a decided edge over your competition, since most people find it easier to place an order by phone than by mail. Furthermore, the incoming WATS line gives the dissatisfied customer a convenient way to let you know what's wrong. And if you don't know, the chances are that you'll eventually lose him. The WATS line is a sophisticated approach, and many people, even today, are impressed with the opportunity to make a free long-distance call. Also, the fact that a company is willing to *pay* for the customer's call says, "We care about you."

Many companies have found the incoming WATS line a very successful way to service customers. It works particularly well for companies that sell consumer products offering warranties and repair contracts. Several manufacturers of major appliances, for instance, provide customers with a toll-free number where they can receive information on local servicing. By directing customers to authorized repairmen, the company insures that the appliance is repaired correctly and that most customer dissatisfaction is nipped in the bud.

What can be accomplished by a WATS line was demonstrated by a large West Coast insurance company that decided to stop issuing disability policies. With the hundreds of agents who had sold only this line no longer representing the company, in many small towns there was no company representation at all.

Before long, the company began receiving complaints from state insurance departments that its policyholders had, in effect, been abandoned. But, as the company explained, "it just wasn't feasible to open local offices in small towns where we had only a handful of policyholders—certainly not enough to warrant the additional overhead." In fact, the reason the company had discontinued the disability line in the first place was that poor claim experience had already made the policy unprofitable.

The solution was an incoming WATS line. In a letter that went to every policyholder, the company gave the 800 number and encouraged policyholders to use it any time they had a question or needed claim service. Clients were also asked to attach the number to their policies, so they could find it in the event of disability. Furthermore, the number was printed on every premium-due notice.

Prior to installing the WATS line, the company had been experiencing a high lapse ratio in its "abandoned" towns. Because a higher percentage of healthy policyholders were letting their policies lapse, this was a cause for real concern. But with the incoming WATS line, the lapse ratio declined noticeably.

"It was just a matter of showing our clients that we cared about them," explained a company vice president. "Now we give the WATS line number to all of our policyholders as a matter of policy."

BEING ACCESSIBLE TO YOUR CUSTOMER

Many a customer has been heard to say, "There was always a salesman there to sell me, but as soon as it came to service, where did all the salesmen go?" The common complaint is that many companies are more eager to sell than to offer service. And, judging from the practices of some firms, there is truth in this charge. To hassle a customer by putting him through a tedious obstacle course is nonsensical, but unfortunately it's the rule, not the exception, in many companies.

Bill Bresnan, the president of Teleprompter, the nation's largest cable television company, feels quite strongly about having the company's local managers accessible to the customer. "Some time ago, a Teleprompter system in a particular city had a public relations problem—an image of not caring about the customers," he says. "For some reason, we were coming across like a utility company. You know, the only cable TV in town." To reverse the situation, management had the system manager take the door of his office off the hinges! What could be a better way of saying that his door was always open? As a further affirmation of this attitude, the manager allowed the newspapers to print his night line number, the private line to his office that bypassed the switchboard. "Not a whole lot of people called," Bill says, "but knowing that he was open to the calls impressed our customers."

When Bill noticed several years ago that many system managers had their home phone numbers unlisted so they wouldn't receive complaints or crank calls at home, he put out a directive. "It said that if they wanted to work for us, they had to be available. They now have their phone numbers listed, and of course, so do I. People have to know we're accessible, not locked up in some isolation chamber."

An excellent example of a salesperson who believes in being accessible is Bettye Hardeman of Atlanta, Georgia. Bettye sold $17.5 million in residential real estate in 1979, and is believed to be the nation's number one residential agent. Bettye firmly understands the necessity of generating referrals and repeat business in the real estate field, and she knows this can be accomplished only by giving service to her clients. "After I sell a home," Bettye says, "I tell my clients to feel free to call me if they ever need anything. I explain to them that I might be too busy to keep on calling them, but that I don't want them to hesitate to call me. I tell them, 'Now, I work long hours, so I'm not always going to be there when you call. But my answering service will give me the message, and I'll get back to you as soon as I can.'"

Bettye's experience, like that of the Teleprompter system managers who listed their phone numbers, is that she doesn't actually get a great many calls. But she believes that the fact that clients know she is available is important. "It's the *offer* that really counts," she insists.

As Bettye says, nobody can be available to incoming calls all the time. For this reason, every salesperson should make sure his calls are received in a way that will not alienate the caller.

Unfortunately, not all people in business share the same philosophy as Bill Bresnan and Bettye Hardeman that they should be accessible to customers. Too often, executives isolate themselves from callers, and the customer is routed through an endless series of other people before being connected. In some cases, even the most persistent caller cannot get through at all. The result is that when the customer finally does get through after having been subjected to the company's "chain of command," he will be disgruntled and in a highly disagreeable mood!

If, for some reason, the individual who can help a caller is not available, the receptionist should courteously extend her assistance by saying, "I'm sorry, but Mr. Smith is not available at the moment. Would you like to hold? Or would it be more convenient for him to call you back?" If the customer says he will hold, the receptionist must check back frequently: "Mr. Smith is still on the other line. Would you like to continue to hold?" Bear in mind that every minute on hold seems like five minutes to the caller!

When the caller chooses to leave a number, it is Mr. Smith's responsibility to return the call immediately. If he cannot, his secretary should call back for him to explain why (perhaps he has a previous commitment) and say that he will be returning the call as soon as possible.

HANDLING COMPLAINTS

Regardless of how well you do your business, sooner or later you're going to have a dissatisfied customer call to complain. Whether you're at fault or the customer is simply a habitual complainer is not the issue. Being right is not important. What does matter is how the customer feels after he talks to you. He must be handled tactfully so you don't lose a customer!

It stands to reason that a customer who calls to complain is likely to be upset. So the first stage in handling him is to attempt to calm him down. You do this by sympathizing. Express your regret for what has gone wrong and explain that you are concerned and want to find a solution. Once a customer hears that you *care,* that you do not want to fight but to help, he will relax. After all, it's difficult to scream and shout at someone who is obviously on your side. Once you show the customer that you care, you are no longer "the bad guy" but a friend.

The second stage in handling a complaint is to understand it clearly. While this sounds simple, it can sometimes take a lot of work to get the facts out of a confused and upset customer. Listen carefully. Ask all the questions you have to in order to identify the problem: who, what, when, where, why, how? Be specific, and make notes while you talk. Listen and question until you know exactly what the complaint is about.

The third stage is verification. Make sure you really have heard correctly. Feed back the information and check out your understanding. If you have been listening carefully, and can verify that you understand, you are ready to adjust the problem.

Certain complaints are more or less standard and can be resolved immediately. More often, you will want some time to check details or discuss a decision with somebody else. If you have to leave the complaint unresolved, arrange a time to call the party back. The longer the complaint is unsettled, the more upset the customer will become. But make certain that whatever time you set is feasible, because it is absolutely imperative that you call him back when you said you would. If for some reason you don't have a solution by that time, call anyway and explain what you have done and why you need more time.

A complaining call that is handled with this kind of attentive courtesy will result in a satisfied customer—and in additional sales. The customer will know you care about him, and he will want more than ever to do business with you. When you hear an angry voice on the phone, don't shy away from it. If you do, you will not only lose this person's business, but you will lose through word of mouth the goodwill that is your most valuable asset. Always remember that the person who is pleased with the way you handled his problem will become your most loyal customer.

Bill Bresnan of Teleprompter explains that the cable company believes the proper handling of incoming customer complaints is crucial to its success. "We feel we must constantly let our customers know we care about them. We work very hard at making sure that every person in our organization knows exactly how to handle customer inquiries on the telephone. If a customer calls in with a complaint and it isn't handled satisfactorily, he may decide to have his service disconnected. So we want our operators to be very good.

"Every telephone operator has what we call our 'bible.' This is a book which is broken down into sections. Whether, for example, it's an inquiry about installation or a customer who is dissatisfied with his reception, the operator can flip to the right section and find out how to handle that call. We think this is very important; if the first contact with a customer or a potential customer is not handled well, there's not going to be another opportunity."

CONCLUSION

In our highly competitive society, extending fine service to the customer is essential. Every top salesperson considers service an integral part of selling. Sometimes, merely *communicating* with your customer by a simple telephone call is an effective way to give service. Furthermore, failure to call him can be deemed a lack of service! The goodwill that a friendly call often creates is invaluable. In other cases, it's crucial to call a customer in order to relay an urgent message.

Servicing by telephone doesn't always mean that you are the one to place the call. Frequently, it's necessary for customers to contact you, and you must establish rapport with your customers so they feel at ease calling you. A WATS line is an excellent way to achieve this goal with out-of-town customers. Many companies have had such good results with their WATS lines that they believe it would be impossible to do out-of-town business on a large scale any other way. These companies feel that it's essential to be accessible to their customers. Accessibility is important to local companies as well, and prompt servicing by telephone is a good way to nip many little problems in the bud. All in all, the telephone is the quickest and most economical means of servicing in the vast majority of cases. Selling and servicing *are* synonymous, and the telephone is an excellent way to do both.

10.

Attitude and Self-Image

Successful telephone salespersons can be male or female, short or tall, thin or plump, young or old, but they all have one thing in common: a good self-image. In fact, you can easily observe that this is true of all successful people. They believe in themselves, and that is the key to success in almost anything. But it is especially true in sales, because *you can't expect anyone else to believe in you unless you believe in you.*

You will never look in the mirror and see a successful salesperson looking back until you have first mentally seen yourself as a successful salesperson. Likewise, the individual at the other end of the telephone line won't visualize you as competent and successful until you see yourself that way.

Is it possible that your positive vibrations can travel over the wires, hundreds or thousands of miles to your prospect? You bet it is. Your enthusiasm and conviction are just as contagious on the telephone as if you were sitting across a desk from the other person. As the nineteenth-century diplomat and writer Edward Bulwer-Lytton said, "Nothing is so contagious as enthusiasm; it moves stones, it charms brutes. Enthusiasm is the genius of sincerity, and truth accomplishes no victories without it." If the telephone had then been invented, he might have added that enthusiasm is capable of traveling around the world through wires. In person or on the telephone, enthusiasm projects your belief in yourself and your product.

BEING PREPARED

If a winning self-image is so important, how do you get one? Isn't it something you get *after* you're successful? Success never hurt anyone's image, but asking which comes first is like asking the old riddle of the chicken and the egg. One thing is certain, though. Success in *anything* depends a great deal on having a positive self-image. So don't just wait for the right mental attitude to evolve; do something about it.

The first step toward a good self-image is making sure you're prepared to sell. This means having full product knowledge as well as knowing *how* to sell the product. After all, it's difficult to think highly of yourself if you don't know what you're talking about. And it's hard to be confident and full of enthusiasm when you stumble over your presentation. Preparation is the price of success; you have to do your homework in advance. You have to know your business so well that you're 100 percent sure there's nothing a customer can ask you that you can't answer. You have to have a presentation you know works, and you have to practice it until it's second nature. Once you've put forth that kind of effort, you'll have the winning self-image to produce fantastic results!

It's important to understand that you must *fully prepare* for your telephone calls; it isn't enough to talk yourself into a sense of false security. While a lot of this chapter will deal with your positive attitude, an attitude isn't enough. You have to have the knowledge that goes with it. A winning self-image is based on dedication and thorough preparation. If you are not fully prepared, you may fool some people, but you'll never really fool yourself. And your self-doubt will tarnish your otherwise winning self-image.

The right self-image is necessary for success, and the important thing to understand is that you don't have to wait for that image to come along. You can develop it by learning your business forward and backward. You are in charge of your own self-image.

BELIEF IN YOUR PRODUCT OR SERVICE

Belief in yourself and belief in your product are interchangeable. It's impossible to have a strong belief in yourself if you don't really respect the value of what you sell. It takes a strong confidence in your product to become excited about it; and when you're excited, others will become excited, too.

Just as enthusiasm is contagious, so are hesitation and doubt, the opposite of enthusiasm. A salesperson who lacks confidence in his product transmits that feeling over the wires. The prospect tends to mimic him and to become uncertain. He, too, loses confidence and becomes less and less capable of making a decision. He, too, has doubts about the product. When the salesperson lacks confidence and hesitates to ask for the order, the prospect will also hem and haw and hesitate to make a buying decision.

When you believe in your product, you relay a strong message to your client that it is in his best interest to make a buying decision. In such an atmosphere, positive vibrations are sent over the wires, and the prospect becomes confident, enthusiastic, and decisive. With conviction, you will feel confident in asking for an order, because you *know* your customer will benefit from the product. And again he will mimic you—this time in a positive way.

Preparation leads to belief in your product. Belief in your product leads to confident, enthusiastic presentations—and sales. And making sales never hurt anyone's self-image! A successful stockbroker, for example, must believe in an investment himself before he recommends it to his client. He must do his homework so *he* fully understands the value of the company. He will want to study the company's return on equity, return on capital, price-earnings multiple, and compound growth rate. He will study the research recommendation in detail, and he'll also speak to the analyst. He'll review annual reports as well as the quarterly reports. By doing his homework, he will become enthusiastic. His knowledge will create confidence in both his product and himself.

One of the best signs of your belief in your product is that *you own it yourself.* When you are selling consumer-oriented products, if you don't own your own product, then you certainly don't have enough conviction to make a really effective presentation. If you sell something to companies, such as computer services or heavy equipment, ask yourself, "If *I* were the customer, would I buy this product over the competitors'?" If you don't believe in it, why should anyone else? As a very successful life insurance agent once confided, "Until I actually carried a million-dollar policy on my own life, I had great difficulty convincing anybody else to be insured for a million."

CONDITIONING YOURSELF

While preparation and conviction are essential to your confidence, you can also work directly on your mental image of yourself. A successful Beverly Hills real estate agent who makes cold calls to potential listers and buyers via telephone every morning has discovered how to do this.

This agent prefers to make her calls from her home, since there are too many distractions in her office. The evening before, she makes up a calling agenda, so that she doesn't have to stop, look up numbers, and try to figure out what she was going to call the individual about. "If I worked that way," she says, "I'd be mentally exhausted in half an hour, and I'd make only a fraction of the calls I make now." Two hours each weekday morning are faithfully devoted to making calls; she has already done all the homework.

While she believes in preparation, this agent (who has asked that her name be withheld) thinks there's another important ingredient to her successful self-image. From the time she gets up at seven until she begins her calls at nine, she follows a schedule devoted to making her feel good and look good. After twenty minutes of aerobic dancing, she has a shower followed by a nutritious breakfast. During breakfast she always reads a good book on some aspect of positive thinking. Then, although nobody will see her until she leaves the house at eleven, she carefully puts on makeup and a crisp business suit.

"I could make the calls in my robe," she says, "but I just wouldn't feel the same. I wear my good jewelry, my high-heeled shoes, the whole bit. I look my best and I *feel* my best! I'm already looking forward to my calls, because I planned them the night before. By the time I go through my morning routine and sit down at the phone, I can't wait to sell real estate!"

This agent also has an efficiently arranged desk set up in her home. "I just wouldn't feel professional working at the kitchen table," she says. Many salespeople are as aware as she is of the importance of a good environment. A Chicago broker states that his agents spend a major portion of their time in the office on the telephone. "Therefore," he says, "I really put a lot of money into decorating the offices. We have a sophisticated telephone system, ready reference devices, and efficient lighting. I believe our people feel important when they work in this kind of atmosphere, and they generate that feeling over the telephone. You'll see real estate offices that are downright depressing. Now, how can an agent feel confident and enthusiastic under those conditions? He's working under a constant handicap. I think a professional environment helps our people feel good about their work and themselves."

Salespersons who have that positive attitude soon begin to believe that every single presentation will result in a sale. They anticipate a sale for every call. Realistically, they know that nobody bats 1,000. But they condition themselves to believe that every prospect is the ideal prospect: "He's going to be receptive. I will do business with him!" When you have this kind of attitude, your enthusiasm comes across. You will be able to do business with many prospects that other salespersons fail with, because you won't hesitate to ask for the order and then ask again!

PROJECTING A WINNING SELF-IMAGE

Two salespersons can have the same training and give exactly the same telephone presentation—yet day in and day out one will outproduce the other. Just plain luck? Luck has nothing to do with it. It's how each individual perceives himself that counts. If you think of yourself as a very important person, the other guy will see you as a VIP, too.

A doubting Thomas might say, "This self-image stuff is a bunch of malarkey. One guy just has a better speaking voice and a better delivery." But the truth is, many top telephone salespersons speak with accents, mispronounce words, have gravel voices, and so on. All else being equal, of course it's an advantage to sound like a radio announcer. Every telephone salesperson should work on improving his voice, a subject we'll cover in Chapter 12, "Speaking Effectively." But if you lack natural talent, you can still be effective, because *it's how you project yourself that counts.*

By and large, your sense of your own importance will determine whether or not your telephone prospect develops a positive image of you. In person, you might come across as a VIP by wearing an expensive suit and having a distinguished profile. But on the telephone, a prospect does not have an opportunity to see you. He must form a mental image based on how you come across. His visualization will depend, to a great extent, on your own self-image. *He will tend to see you as you see yourself.* And very often the image he forms will not look a bit like you! How many times, for example, have you met someone in person after knowing him only over the telephone? When that happens, you may often be startled. The individual is very different than you imagined. He may be older or taller or heavier. He may dress differently than you thought he would. When this happens, you tend to think the telephone image was "wrong." But perhaps what we *see* is a facade, and the telephone image is the real thing—a more accurate representation of what the person is really like. As we know, appearances can be deceiving.

Consciously or unconsciously, a salesperson has an image of himself; and that image is conveyed over the telephone. The run-of-the-mill salesperson often seems to think of himself as "just a salesman," and as a result he is timid in his approach and hesitant in his presentation. His unconscious mental image seems to be that of a dog begging the prospect to please throw him a bone. The successful salesperson, however, sees himself as important. When he's talking to a prospect, he isn't nervous about taking up the prospect's time; he knows that *his* time is just as valuable as the prospect's. He knows that what he's saying is as important as anything the prospect is going to hear that day. He believes, "This guy needs my product. I'm doing him a favor to call." His self-image is confident and important. And whether you're a novice or an experienced salesperson, you too must think of yourself as a VIP. Only then can you project that image to the person on the other end of the wire.

A POSITIVE MENTAL ATTITUDE

An important ingredient of every salesperson's self-esteem is the confidence that he *can* sell. He approaches every call with enthusiasm, because he believes the individual needs the product and will appreciate hearing about it. When he gets a no, he isn't discouraged, because he knows that's part of the overall picture and he will sell the next one.

Richard Schultz says he can almost always tell which of National Revenue's salespeople are effective on the telephone just by watching how they dial the phone. "Good salesmen *attack* the phone," he says. "They make one call right after another, boom, boom, boom! The person who dislikes telephone selling and lacks confidence picks up the phone slowly. He'll punch out those numbers in slow motion. You can tell from his expression that he's just hoping to get a busy signal. When he does, he sighs, 'Well, it's just a game of numbers,' and he's relieved to hang up.

"Then he dilly-dallies around, and after a while he figures he has to make another call. But the top salesman has everything nearby, so he doesn't have to stop between calls. As soon as he's through with one call, he's moving on to the next one. He's excited about his product and he believes in himself, so he can't wait to tell people about the good thing he has for them."

When you have prepared until you're an expert in your field, and you know your presentation backward and forward, a positive attitude like this comes naturally. You're like a speaker who knows he's going to make a good speech. He can't wait to get up in front of his audience and deliver it. Because he is well prepared, he knows he can't miss. Likewise, you must prepare yourself to sell effectively on the telephone, and you too will win the right to a receptive audience.

Preparing yourself to sell is similar to an athlete getting into top condition before an athletic event. He, too, does his "homework," and whether he wins or loses will depend greatly upon how well he trained. A professional boxer, for example, will get himself into tip-top shape before a championship fight. And in the process, he will get so psyched up that he *knows* he's going to win! He must be positive beyond a doubt. He must enter the ring with complete confidence. If he doesn't, he will begin to pull his punches, and his hesitation will become a tremendous handicap. A salesperson with self-doubt works under an equally great handicap. You too must get yourself into tip-top shape by knowing your business backward and forward—and cultivating the attitude that when you get on the phone you're going to make every sale!

The super salesperson honestly believes that anyone who turns him down is making a mistake. And because he's so well prepared and enthusiastic, he can say to himself, "I know he's going to buy, and he knows I know he's going to buy. Pretty soon *he knows he's going to buy.*" A person with this attitude automatically projects enthusiasm and conviction. It's no wonder he does so well selling on the telephone. He *knows* he's going to.

A positive mental attitude goes hand in hand with a positive self-image. If you become discouraged easily, if you really expect to be turned down, ask yourself how you perceive yourself. Do you think you're "just a salesperson" or do you see yourself as an expert in your field? It's impossible to maintain a positive mental attitude unless you consider yourself a professional person with a philosophy—a concept—and an important service to offer your prospect. As we discussed in Chapter 5, a stockbroker shouldn't think of himself as selling stocks and bonds. He's selling a concept which represents a value to his client. The investment he recommends is the vehicle that will realize a value for his client.

Likewise, a life insurance agent shouldn't think in terms of selling a contract to pay X amount of dollars in the event of the client's death. He's selling ideas. He may suggest, for instance, that the proceeds from the policy will educate the prospect's children, or fund a buy-sell agreement between two partners, or provide funds for estate purposes. By the same token, a salesperson whose product is vibrating chairs that retail for $1,000 isn't selling an expensive chair with a built-in motor; he's selling therapeutic equipment that relieves tension, backaches, and arthritic pain. He's selling comfort and relaxation.

IBM's Buck Rodgers, senior vice president in charge of worldwide marketing, perhaps sums it up best when he says, "We supply a solution to our customer's problems. We're not selling a product, but instead what the product will do." He continues: "For example, if I say to you, 'I've got something that will make your job easier, it's going to reduce your cost, and it's a way to allow you to give better service to your customers,' you're going to be interested in hearing what I've got to tell you. And that's what it's all about! While there are people who fear a computer and think in terms of its impersonal nature, you've got to look at what the machine actually does. For example, it can help save lives. It can mechanize our libraries and make them more useful. It can aid in the decision-making process. It can free people from repetitive work. It can make somebody's job more exciting and more meaningful. There are, in fact, countless ways a computer can serve mankind."

When you have trouble feeling positive about your calls, remind yourself that the prospect needs you. You can solve his problem; without your help, he can't solve it. With this kind of self-image, you will have no trouble cultivating an enthusiastic attitude. You're no longer "just a salesperson."

ASKING FOR THE ORDER WITH CONFIDENCE

Your winning self-image is important every step of the way. But nowhere is self-confidence more vital than in the closing. A confident salesperson will ask for the order with a positive attitude. If he's turned down, he will discuss the objection and ask for the order again.

When you request the order, you must do it with confidence in order to generate confidence in the prospect. He must feel sure that he's doing the right thing. He must believe it would be a mistake not to buy. The confidence he has in his decision will depend largely on the confidence you have when you ask for the order. If you do it confidently, he'll become confident too. It's contagious. You might say, wrapping up the sale, "Jim, that's ten thousand units at nine dollars. I'll have them shipped this afternoon. And let me congratulate you on making a very wise purchase. You're getting an outstanding value." These words, spoken with complete self-confidence, reaffirm the wise decision he has made.

A timid salesperson, on the other hand, can lose the sale even *after* the close, by projecting a losing image. Using the very same wrap-up, he may hem and haw and hesitate: "Er, Jim, let's see, that's, did you say ten thousand units? Mmm, at eight, er, no, nine dollars. Say, ah, how about if I ship them next week?" At this point the prospect will naturally pick up the indecision—the salesperson has suddenly cast doubts on the order. The prospect is likely to interrupt now (at a point where the salesman should not have paused in the first place), and say, "Well, I really don't know what I should do. I'll have to think about this for a while. Maybe check out some other sources. I'll have to shop around." The salesman had the sale and lost it!

CONCLUSION

A winning self-image is essential in order to achieve success in selling. It is perhaps even more important in telephone selling than face-to-face selling, because the prospect's image depends entirely on how he visualizes you. He has not had the opportunity to meet you in person.

Fortunately, your self-image is something you can develop. The first thing you do is learn your business until you are an expert in your field. Next, you must work diligently at developing an effective presentation. Then you practice it until you know you can present your product or service so that anyone will recognize the value. Before making calls, prepare your working environment in any way you can so that your self-image is positive. Do whatever it takes to get psyched up. Kick out the "just a salesperson" image and visualize yourself as a professional. How you see yourself is going to play a big part in what you project to the prospect.

Finally, work on a positive mental attitude. Remember that if you don't succeed with one prospect, you're that much closer to the next sale. Just pick up the receiver and keep on calling. You're an expert, a professional. You *know* you're going to make a sale on this call!

11

How to Sell Yourself
on the Telephone

American free enterprise is the most competitive economic system on earth. Regardless of the field, there isn't a product or service offered that can't be duplicated. The life insurance industry is a good example. Every agent sells policies similar to, if not identical with, the policies every other agent sells—and there are more than 1,800 companies licensed to sell life insurance! The same situation is true in real estate; with multiple-listing services, a number of real estate agents have the opportunity to sell the same properties. Whatever the industry, nobody has a monopoly on a given product or service.

This would make a salesperson's task look hopeless, except for one vital fact: We all have a monopoly on something unique—*ourselves. You* make the difference. The personal attention and service you extend to the client is a significant part of the total package, and in most cases it determines whether he will buy from you or from somebody else. Whatever you sell, don't ever think that your customer isn't buying you when he agrees to the transaction.

Selling oneself is a basic principle that is followed by all successful salespersons. In face-to-face selling, it may involve good grooming, a nice smile, a firm handshake, carefully chosen clothes, even sex appeal. But these physical attributes don't count in telephone selling.

Because of this fact, some novice telephone salespersons tend to underrate the importance of selling themselves. True, on the telephone you have to do it without visual props. Because you are at first "just a voice," you may have to work harder at projecting personality. Just the same, you must sell yourself to achieve maximum results.

BELIEVING IN YOURSELF

You will never convince anybody to believe in you until you do. Likewise, *you will never sell yourself until you are sold on yourself.* When Joe Girard is asked how he sells more automobiles than anyone else in the world, he replies, "I don't have any big secrets. I simply sell the world's best product, that's all. *I sell Joe Girard!"* Joe's objective is to make every customer want to do business with him, and he obviously does a good job at it. For eleven consecutive years, he sold more automobiles and trucks than any other retail salesman anywhere. They were all Chevrolets, a good make representing a good value, but certainly not a product that couldn't be purchased somewhere else. While Joe had a good product, he personally won the customers because *he sold himself.*

The key to this kind of salesmanship is belief. Joe believes in himself. He is convinced that *he* is the best product. And once he was convinced of that fact, it became easy to convince others. On the other hand, if you don't believe in yourself, selling any product is an uphill battle. As we discussed in the last chapter, you really can't expect anyone else to believe in you if you don't believe in yourself.

Believing in yourself does not mean ignoring your product. In fact, your belief in yourself and in your product are interchangeable. When you are enthusiastic about your own capabilities, you will refuse to sell a product you don't believe in. Your conviction about yourself *and* your product will be transmitted, and your prospect will react positively. In the same way, we have continually emphasized the importance of doing your homework so that you know your product backward and forward. When you do, belief in yourself will come naturally.

Perhaps the most important thing to remember is exactly where the sale begins. It doesn't begin with selling the prospect on the product; it doesn't even begin with selling him on yourself. *The sale begins when you sell yourself to you.*

SELLING YOUR COMPANY

In your eagerness to sell yourself and your product, don't forget to sell your company. Often a salesperson believes this tactic will work against him; he wants to win the client's loyalty to himself alone. Such a salesperson is likely to say, "My clients buy me, not the company. It doesn't make any difference what company I represent. If I changed to another company, I'd take my clients with me." This is a serious mistake. Whether it is true or not, it makes better sense to build up your company along with yourself. First, it shows that you're loyal; you don't bite the hand that feeds you. And even in today's fast-paced world, people continue to admire loyalty and see it as a sign of character. On a more practical level, selling your company works to your advantage. Your firm is probably outstanding in one respect or another, perhaps in several ways. If you've got it, flaunt it! Let the customer know why so many clients prefer doing business with your company over the competition. If you overlook doing this, you're likely to be missing out on a very good selling point.

The company is more important in a telephone sales call than in a face-to-face call, because the customer may very well be familiar with your company—but he doesn't know you! Praising your company is an excellent way to establish credibility. For instance, when Tom Jones makes a cold call on a prospect and identifies himself as a Prudential agent, Tom may be a stranger, but the prospect has certainly heard of Prudential. The same is true of IBM, Xerox, Century 21, and thousands of other respected, well-known corporations. If you do represent a well-known company, take advantage of it; use it as a selling point. In many cases, the company's good name will be your ticket to selling a prospect who might otherwise refuse to make a transaction over the phone.

Perhaps you represent a firm which is not exactly a household word. In this case, you *must* sell your company. Since the prospect is not familiar with it, you must relieve any doubts he might have. If the firm is small, use that, too, as a selling point: "Mr. Brown, let me tell you that we may be small, but we won't be for very long. We're 100 percent committed to giving service. And because we're small, we're light on our feet. As a matter of fact, you can get personal service from the president himself! Just call us at any time. His door is always open."

As you can see, whether your company is just starting out or is a national giant, it is always to your advantage to sell the company as a way of selling yourself. Your company's strength, quality, and reliability are important selling points. And selling your company makes *you* look good because you had the good judgment to select a top company—and they, in turn, selected you!

One of the best ways you have of selling yourself is to make available to your clients the total resources of your company. Many firms have much to offer a client beyond just the transaction. In the securities business, for instance, the firm's library is one of them. There may be some information you can obtain regarding your client's competitors which would be of benefit to him. Emphasize to your clients that you have a team of experts who work with you, representing many years of experience and substantial financial resources. Make sure that they realize that they are dealing not just with you but with a major organization. You're the conductor. You have an orchestra of dozens of people—experts in securities, government bonds, convertible bonds, short-term and long-term municipals, short-term and long-term corporates, commercial paper, CD's, Fanny Maes—it's a team effort. As the conductor, you are always evaluating the various areas so that you may project a total picture to your clients.

Emphasize that the full resources of your company are at their disposal because of their relationship with you. You make this available because *you want to help them.* This is the key. Stress that over and over. In essence, you are saying to the client, "Look, our relationship is not only one of investing for you, but one of helping you in any way we can." It's important to realize that a stockbroker is bound to have some transactions with his clients that will not be successful. But he won't necessarily lose a client because an investment turned sour. Instead, he'll lose a client because of an unsuccessful relationship.

PERSONALIZING YOUR PRESENTATION

Talk to almost any executive of a major corporation, and he will tell you, "This is a people business." It doesn't matter what his product is—insurance, heavy machinery, computers—he understands that people are what make the industry. And regardless of what you sell, you're in a people business too. With this in mind, you must personalize your telephone calls so that the individual at the other end of the line knows he's important to you. You must show him he's more than a number on a computer card. You must demonstrate that you understand and can identify with his special needs.

National Revenue representatives are trained to be specialists when they call on prospects. "The first thing our salesperson does," Richard Schultz explains, "is tell the prospect who referred him, and of course it is someone the prospect knows or someone in the same field. Then, early in the presentation, the salesperson will say, 'I specialize in the jewelry business.' Naming your specialty is very important. It establishes rapport and it shows that you know how to deal with his particular problems.

"Our representative will also let the prospect know that our company has been endorsed by the Jewelers Association (local, state, or national, whatever the situation is). Again, an endorsement gives credibility. To further personalize the presentation, our salesperson will call the prospect by his first name—several times. He will try to talk as if they were talking face to face. We don't want him to come across as some stranger who has nothing better to do with his time than make cold calls.

"We also make a point of talking the prospect's language," Richard continues. "We don't talk to a doctor about bad debts. We talk about 'delinquent debtor patients,' and 'the transfusion of cash flow' into his practice. We tell him, 'National Revenue doesn't alienate the debtor patients, but rather we educate them to the fact that they owe you an obligation. We bring them back into your practice. They pay you what they owe you and continue receiving the medical care that they need.' Likewise, when we talk to the owner of an insurance agency, we will talk about 'earned premiums.' I don't care what the prospect does. If he's a hod carrier, then I specialize in hod carriers. I want him to know we speak his language, because that shows we have some degree of expertise in the type of work he does."

HAVING A SENSE OF HUMOR

Regardless of what you sell, injecting humor at the right time into your telephone selling is appropriate. Now, this doesn't mean you should become a comedian or start off your presentation with a dirty joke. But when the timing is right, a sense of humor can be effective.

Humor can humanize an otherwise dull conversation, and it tends to relax people. It also makes doing business with you more enjoyable—and there's no rule that says your clients can't enjoy doing business with you. In dealing with a somewhat cool prospect, the right touch of wit or humor can be an effective icebreaker. But a word of caution: Use discretion. Don't overdo it. Be sensitive to your prospect's personality. While most people enjoy a laugh, there are those who are all business and are determined to stay that way. There's a place for humor in business when it's used at the right time; but when it's used improperly, it can backfire.

GENERATING REPEAT BUSINESS
(RESELLING YOURSELF)

In the majority of businesses, as mentioned before, 20 percent of the customers will generate 80 percent of the sales volume. If this is the case in your situation, doesn't it make sense to spend some extra time with your existing clients and *resell* yourself? While it is highly important to prospect for new accounts on a daily basis, there is probably a gold mine among your present customers. And since these accounts can be so lucrative, it is certainly worthwhile to concentrate on them. They are your bread and butter.

How about going over your list of steady customers and requalifying them? Resell yourself as a person who is willing to give them service and might be able to offer them something else. In requalifying a client, and talking to him about his needs, you may be surprised to discover that there are areas of his business he could be giving you but isn't. Until you have had a friendly, probing talk with a client, never assume that you know everything about him. If you're a stockbroker, you may learn that a client has a need for tax-free bonds but is purchasing them through another source. If you're an insurance agent, many of your clients will need additional insurance sooner or later, and a more aggressive salesperson may be getting the bulk of the premium dollars. If you are in real estate, and you have sold a client a residential property, requalification may reveal that this individual also buys investment real estate on a regular basis—and in dollar amounts much greater than the value of the home he purchased through you. In short, you'll probably be surprised at how much additional business you could be doing with the clients you already have. Take the time to sell yourself all over again—and then generate additional sales.

CONCLUSION

Every salesperson sells a package that includes his product, his company, and *himself.* Your competition may have a comparable product, and a company that equals yours, but *you* are unique. If you are willing to market yourself, and extend yourself, you will be offering something to your clients that they can't get anywhere else. Remember, *you* are a very important ingredient in the total package; don't ever leave that ingredient out. If you want to be a super salesperson, you must sell the world's best product—sell yourself.

12.

Speaking Effectively

Throughout this book we have emphasized the importance of such intangibles as conviction, enthusiasm, and self-confidence. In this chapter we will cover the nitty-gritty details of how you can use your speech to convey those intangible qualities. But may we add that this chapter is not a course on effective speaking. We cannot offer "miracle cures" that will instantly give you the perfect diction and pearlike tones of a radio announcer. We do, however, have some basic suggestions which will help you add interest and conviction to your presentation. And these tips do not require that you hire a speech coach or therapist. With a little practice, you can apply them immediately.

How you say it is paramount in telephone selling. As we have stressed in previous chapters, you cannot rely on non-verbal communication during a telephone conversation. You can't clench your fist and pound it on the table to emphasize a point. Nor will a shrug or a faint smile help you overcome an objection. On the telephone there's no such thing as eye contact to help establish rapport. You must depend on your voice to deliver your message. Other than *what* you say, *how you say it is the best thing you've got going for you.*

It's been said that "you only get one chance to make a first impression." In person, appearances make a difference. In person, you present to the prospect a total package that includes your physical build, your clothing, your smile, and so on. An attractive salesperson who oozes charm may not be handicapped by an unpleasant voice in a personal sales call. But on the telephone, your first impression is entirely dependent on how you speak.

In fact, there seems to be a thing such as "a good telephone personality." Did you ever know someone who could always get a blind date on the telephone but never made a hit with the girls in person? "Well, he has a telephone personality," people say. In person, perhaps his image is tarnished by such offensive mannerisms as having a habit of scratching himself, a nervous tic, or bad breath. But on the telephone, only his smooth voice transmits his image. In his case, the telephone allows him to use his best asset. For others, their telephone voices are liabilities. But the fact remains that you do come across differently on the telephone than in person.

Speaking traits which would be relatively insignificant in a personal encounter can be all-important on the telephone. Your prospects are not likely to tell you that you annoy them by talking too fast, or using a high, raspy tone. A good way to find out is to listen to yourself. For analyzing your speaking voice, you can use the same tapes you used to work on your presentation. These tapes are especially good, because at the time you made them you were conscious of what you were saying but probably weren't paying too much attention to how you sounded. In order to carefully analyze how you use your voice, you should be working with a recording.

If you are totally satisfied with your production, then you can skip the rest of this chapter. But most of us have plenty of room for improvement. In working with your own speech habits, avoid being too demanding on yourself. Your purpose is first to deliver your message so that the prospect receives it clearly. Second, you want to do it in such a way that you don't annoy him by your delivery and work against yourself. You want your voice to carry your enthusiasm for your product or service, and your conviction. And you want your voice to help you create a transaction. You can do all this without developing the skills of a professional speaker. For your purposes as a telephone salesperson, it is enough to be clear, pleasant, and convincing.

SPEAKING CLEARLY

Obviously, a telephone salesperson's first goal should be to deliver the presentation clearly enough that the prospect can easily understand it. Unfortunately, this isn't as natural as it might sound. There are those who mumble and consistently mispronounce words. Others naturally talk in a low voice that is hardly audible. Some speak so quickly that half the words are lost. In these cases, the prospect may despair of ever understanding the message and simply hang up.

The first and easiest thing to control is the rate of speed. Most people speak too fast on the telephone. One of the pitfalls of knowing your presentation thoroughly is that you may "recite" it at an unnaturally fast rate, thereby confusing the listener. Important selling points should often be delivered with deliberate slowness so that the prospect doesn't miss them. It is possible, however, to speak too slowly. If you do, the prospect will become impatient and wonder when in the world you will get to the point. In listening to your own presentation, analyze your rate of speed. Are you boring the prospect? Are you confusing him? Or are you speaking at a moderate rate of speed that is easy to understand?

Volume is equally important, and is also relatively easy to control. Many people tend to speak too loudly on the telephone. Perhaps they feel they have to speak out because the other person isn't in the room. But remember, a New York to San Francisco call usually does not require a louder speaking voice than a call to another person in the same office building. If you've ever seen someone holding a phone away from his ear and grimacing, you know how irritating an overly loud telephone voice can be.

As a salesperson, however, you want to come across as forceful and decisive. Given a choice, it is better to err in the direction of speaking too loudly than it is to speak too softly. If you use a very low voice, you run the risk that the prospect won't hear you at all! Moreover, a soft voice sometimes projects an image of meekness and a lack of conviction—certainly not desirable qualities for a salesperson.

Speaking clearly also involves good pronunciation. Obviously, it is imperative that the other person know exactly what you have said. You certainly don't want a five to sound like a nine; that can have grave consequences! Clear pronunciation makes it possible for your prospect to concentrate on the message. On the other hand, if you mumble and mispronounce words, he must occupy himself with trying to figure out what you said. When that happens, your presentation has lost its effectiveness. If your analysis of your voice tells you that you speak indistinctly, consider slowing down; most of the time mumbling and poor pronunciation are a result of nervous haste.

If you hear a stutter or other speech difficulty in your tapes, consider whether professional therapy is in order. This book is no cure-all, and even minor speech problems require practice, practice, and more practice. We would question whether *any* book can provide enough help to substitute for a trained professional where a serious speech difficulty exists. You can't just read a chapter and overcome a lifetime disability.

USING VARIATION

The quickest way to improve your presentation is to add variety to your delivery. When a presentation is given at the same rate of speed and in the same monotonous tone of voice, the most exciting new product in the world will seem dull.

Rate and volume are not just varied any which way. By speaking slowly, you place emphasis on major selling points. By moving more quickly (but not speeding!) over less important features, you signal to the prospect that these issues do not have the same degree of significance. In the same way, either raising or lowering the volume of your voice will call the prospect's attention to what you are saying. A louder voice will tend to convey enthusiasm. A softer voice, on the other hand, tells the prospect, "Now, this is confidential, so listen carefully to what I have to say."

Speech variation gives your presentation that vital touch of *showmanship*. True, you're not there to entertain your clients. But it *is* necessary to keep a prospect's attention. By adding emphasis and variety to your presentation, you provide a dramatic format in which to hold a captive audience. If you sense that your prospects get bored with your presentation it might help you to think of yourself as an actor on stage with the prospect as your audience. You too have a fine script, a presentation you have worked and reworked. But are you getting applause? While a salesperson does not actually get boos or claps, he receives his feedback in terms of sales. You might think of a large order as a standing ovation for an excellent dramatic presentation. In the long run, like an actor, the salesperson receives earnings based on the reception of his audience. So don't be bashful about trying for variety. Put on a good show!

THE PAUSE

One of the most dramatic and effective speaking devices is the pause. Obviously, we are not talking about the haphazard pause of the salesperson who forgets where he is and what he's talking about. But a carefully timed pause adds emphasis to the presentation, and allows you to structure the prospect's response.

As Chapter 13, "Listening," will explain, silence is not a flaw in the conversation. Study any professional speaker—an actor, a clergyman, a politician—and you will notice pauses used deliberately and effectively. On the telephone, however, a pause of just a few seconds seems longer than the same pause in person. At first you may think that you already use pauses. In listening to your tape, pay close attention to them. Are they long enough to let the prospect into the conversation if he wishes to tell you something? Alternatively, are you using pauses to prevent the prospect from breaking into the presentation in inappropriate places? Both uses are legitimate. Don't be afraid to incorporate intentional pauses into your presentation.

An individual who has perfected the use of the pause in his

telephone presentation is Richard Schultz of National Revenue. "A subtle and professional way to get the right effect is to pause in the middle of a sentence," he states. "Why in the middle? Because people won't interrupt in the middle of a thought, whereas they will interrupt if you pause at the end of a thought. This is especially important in the initial approach, when you want to get to the main selling point before you allow the prospect to object or make a hasty decision.

"I learned the technique of pausing in the middle of a sentence by observing John Wayne. He was a master at this. The Duke would say, 'When I talk, one thing I do is always . . . [and he'd pause] . . . end up in the middle of a sentence on a high note so that . . . [and he'd pause again] . . . the man knows that . . . [another pause] . . . I'm not done yet.'

"We teach this technique to our people," Richard says, "so they give a presentation like this: 'John, our company collects delinquent accounts and we do it a little differently than anyone else in the country in that . . . [pause] . . . we give a 100 percent guarantee on the results to our users, John, where . . . [pause] for an unusually low one-time fixed fee, we'll collect any accounts on your books. Now . . . [pause] . . . this is regardless of the age, the size, or the debtor's location, anywhere in the United States. And John . . . [pause] . . . when you submit an account to us, we do all the work and the money is paid directly to you. And if the debtor won't pay . . . [pause] . . . at your discretion we take him to court.' "

In the above example, the pause is used very effectively to (1) hold the prospect's attention and (2) control the interview so there is no interruption. Richard points out that it takes considerable practice with a tape recorder for a salesperson to develop this technique. Again, effective use of the voice is not something you stumble on by accident; it takes practice.

THE TELEPHONE SMILE

While "telephone personality" is impossible to define, it certainly includes an element of friendliness. Perhaps the easiest way to come across as a cheerful, friendly person is to have a big smile on your face—whether the prospect can see that smile or not! The feeling behind a smile is transmitted to the tonal qualities of your voice. Many people who want to sound friendly never think of smiling while talking on the telephone, and the other person can sense it. Why? Because without a smile, they sound unfriendly.

Many companies feel so strongly about the importance of having their telephone people sound friendly that they place mirrors in front of them with the word SMILE printed boldly right on the glass surface. This serves as a constant reminder to smile while you talk to the other person, and it's hard to sound unfriendly while you're smiling.

CONCLUSION

In this chapter, our objective has been to help you develop awareness of your telephone speaking habits. We have purposely avoided getting into the fine details of effective speaking, because volumes have been written on this subject. Yet, a book on telephone selling which did not stress the importance of speaking habits would certainly be deficient. We hope that some of the real advantages and possibilities of effective speech may interest you in pursuing the subject further.

Just as an actor rehearses his script, a salesperson must work to develop a really effective presentation. Although a good actor's performance looks natural on stage, remember, he didn't perfect that role by merely getting in front of an audience and reading it. Achieving variety and interest takes work. Likewise, a salesman cannot achieve an effective presentation by merely going through the motions. Such a presentation will inevitably be detected by a prospect as being "canned" and therefore will produce a negative reaction.

You can't expect to give a great presentation just because you have written out the right words. Like an actor, you have to rehearse, carefully considering how you use your voice to add impact to what you're saying. Practice in front of a mirror, on a tape recorder, with friends and associates. Work on one thing at a time, and then put it together. Triple-space your presentation and mark it to remind yourself where to speak softly, where to pause, and where to come in LOUD and CONFIDENT. Soon your presentation will have personality and excitement. It will come alive!

A few weeks later, tape your new presentation and compare it to the old one. You'll be amazed at the difference. Although you used the same word-for-word presentation, you'll hardly recognize the "old" you.

13.
Listening

Effective salesmanship is based on communication, and communication is a two-way street. While you must present your product or service convincingly, the ability to listen is equally important in the selling process. A professional salesperson must understand how his prospect thinks and feels; otherwise he cannot properly service him. In telephone selling, this understanding can only be gained through listening.

On the telephone, the skill of listening is obviously more important than in face-to-face selling, because what the prospect says is your only feedback. Unlike the in-person sales representative, you cannot see your prospect's facial expressions or body language. There are no visible buying signals, such as reaction to a visual sales aid, participation in a demonstration, or concentration in reading a brochure. A telephone salesperson can observe buying signals only by listening to what the prospect says and how he says it.

This lack of visual feedback may seem a major handicap. However, that does not have to be the case. The astute telephone salesperson develops a sixth sense, similar to a blind person's ability to "see" things by sound. Once your skill in detecting buying signals through effective listening is developed, you will be able to diagnose your prospect's reactions with a great degree of proficiency and precision.

WHY MOST SALESPERSONS DON'T LISTEN

In the popular stereotype, the salesperson is a super talker—a carnival barker type, a man with a silver tongue. While this image is false, many salespersons act as if they believed it. They operate under the erroneous impression that salesmanship is the ability to persuade another person through a talkathon. Striving to fit this role, they consider any pause in the conversation to represent a flaw in their presentation. Nothing could be further from the truth. A deliberate pause, or a moment of silence at the right time, is a potent selling technique in the hands of the skilled salesperson.

Most salespersons suffer from this misconception to some extent. Typically, they get *telephone fright* (yes, it's something like stage fright) whenever there is a silence. They feel uneasy if nobody is talking. Something must be wrong! Actually, salespersons are not the only people who think this way. Ours is a very verbal society. If you observe how people behave at social gatherings, you will see that silence makes most people very uncomfortable. Somehow, many of us believe that the greater the amount of talking, the more successful the conversation will be.

This problem is intensified for the typical salesperson, because he is preoccupied by what he must *say*. Consequently, he fails to *listen*. This is why we have stressed the planned sales presentation, practiced to the point of unconscious competence. A fully prepared salesperson can listen without losing the thread of the presentation. He is willing to allow the prospect to express himself, and able to hear the objections or the buying signals in what the prospect is saying.

As the old adage goes, "Speech is silver, silence golden." Never be hesitant about allowing a silence to occur in your conversation with a prospect. Silence represents understanding and patience. It demonstrates that you are interested in hearing the other person's point of view. It helps establish a relationship, because everyone loves a good listener. Silence gives the prospect the opportunity to speak. A non-stop presentation which closes the prospect out will

LISTENING ♨ *139*

only antagonize him and create a barrier to building a good sales-person-client relationship.

LISTENING TO THE CUSTOMER

Remember that the customer wants to talk too. If you listen, you are sure to learn something about him. As the saying goes, listening is the greater part of learning. Far too many salespersons use their presentation time talking instead of listening. As a result, they don't know what the prospect wants. If they would listen, the prospect would tell them!

Listening does not just mean passively receiving. *You must demonstrate that you care.* This means you must listen sympathetically. Some of the customer's objections may seem nonsensical, and others irrelevant, but you have to extend your courtesy to his concerns. Although you may inwardly judge that an objection is not real, it must nevertheless be treated with the utmost sincerity.

We have devoted a great deal of time to discussing the importance of overcoming objections in order to create the transaction. But we have also stressed that simply overcoming objections is not enough. You must convey to the prospect that you are really concerned about his thinking. Your objective is not to counter all objections and "win" the conversation. Instead, you must listen to your prospect and empathize with him. An understanding ear will do considerably more to win him over than a smooth, quick-talking answer.

Everybody loves a good listener. And nowhere is the skill of listening more important than in telephone selling. When you extend the ultimate courtesy of listening to the other person, you let him know that you care about him. Instead of telling him what he ought to buy, you are showing him that you want to know what he needs. While this willingness to listen may sound natural, it is not. The vast majority of salespersons are more interested in talking than listening. Undoubtedly, this attitude is one of the major reasons why so many people are hostile to telephone salespersons.

LISTENING TO YOURSELF

Nobody can deny that listening is an important ingredient in telephone selling, and most of us think in terms of listening to the other person. However, one of the most productive methods you can use to improve your presentation is to begin to *listen to yourself.* If you have never recorded your presentation and played it back, you will probably be astonished—and perhaps disappointed —at what you hear. We have often seen salespeople groan and shake their heads and ask, "Do I *really* do that?" But if you begin listening to yourself, your presentation will improve by leaps and bounds.

It is certainly possible—and desirable—to listen to yourself as you give an actual presentation. But this is not ideal, since you will be busy listening to the prospect too and controlling the interview. The best way to monitor yourself is to *role-play* with another salesperson, a friend, or a family member. Tape your presentation, and throw yourself into the part. In listening to the recording, put yourself in the prospect's position. Do you sound like a person *you* would want to do business with? Are you sympathetic? Do you have conviction? *Do you listen?*

Make a list of the strengths as well as the weaknesses you find in your presentation. It is sometimes difficult to be candid with yourself during this process, but it's well worth the effort. While most people find several areas that need improvement, it is usually best to confine yourself to one significant weakness at a time and to work diligently on that. This kind of tough self-analysis will lead to vast improvements. And bear in mind that listening to your own presentation and improving it is an ongoing process that should continue periodically throughout your career.

Sure, it takes effort. But listening to yourself is a very effective way to improve your skills. With practice, you'll find that you can learn to listen to yourself with detachment, and you will begin to be pleased by the improvements you hear in each new tape. Sales-persons who are not willing to make this effort are resigning themselves to be members of the vast army of people who settle for mediocrity.

Another excellent way to listen to yourself is to interact with other people within your industry. This can mean meeting with members of your own organization—both local and out-of-town people. It can include attending conferences and seminars. In many cases, the most beneficial part of such get-togethers is the exchange of ideas during one-to-one discussions. So stick around after the formal talks and get to know others who attend these functions.

Also, be sure to participate as a speaker on the subject of selling whenever you get the chance. When you speak before your peers about your own philosophy and strategy, you will learn a tremendous amount. There is no better way to refresh your mind on your own beliefs and convictions. Preparing to speak publicly forces you to clarify your routine activities, and perhaps to see the possibilities for improved efficiency and more effective selling. And talking with enthusiasm about what you do is one of the best ways there is to generate enthusiasm—within yourself as well as your audience. The individual who finds ways to attend conferences and to speak on a regular basis will perceive himself more clearly and become an even more effective salesperson as a result.

GETTING YOUR PROSPECT INTO THE ACT

Although listening carefully to your prospect's comments is vital, the professional salesperson will go a step further. He will make every effort to draw the prospect into the conversation. Some people love to talk and will freely tell you their reactions to the presentation, but many others need encouragement. Remember, the only way you have of observing your prospect's reaction is to listen to him. Therefore, if he doesn't voice an opinion, you have to draw him out.

Throughout this book, we have demonstrated how top salespersons all over the country are doing this very thing throughout their presentations. Often an "opinion question" is asked: "Would you agree that . . ." "What do *you* think about . . ." "Does this philosophy make sense?" "How has your experience been with such-and-such?" Notice that these questions often call for more than a simple yes or no response. And if a question may be merely answered yes, a tactful pause permits the prospect an opportunity to explain why he agrees.

The prospect cannot enter the conversation when you are talking. At times, you must remain silent and allow him the opportunity to fully answer your questions. Often the prospect who is given this opening will end up selling himself. During a warm-up session, you should remind yourself that he may need time to formulate his thoughts. It is not necessary to speak out immediately when he finishes a sentence. He may have an additional thought to express, which you will not hear unless you allow a brief pause. A good rule of thumb is to count slowly to five after he stops talking. Then you can have your turn to speak!

BEING A RESPONSIVE LISTENER

There is a definite difference between listening on the telephone and listening in person. When a prospect is speaking on the telephone, you can't look at him attentively and nod your head occasionally to show him that you understand. When he is talking, he may interpret total silence as a sign of boredom or unconcern. So you have to get into the act. Concentrate on what he is saying. Without interrupting his flow, make such comments as "Yes, I agree," "I follow you," "That's interesting," and so on. But do this in a way that allows him to continue talking and expressing his thoughts. These responsive comments signal to the prospect that you are paying attention to what he is saying.

By letting him know that he has your full, undivided attention, you're showing him that you care. And by all means, don't allow anyone to interrupt you while you're on the telephone with a prospect. Such an interruption would be equivalent to a salesperson in a face-to-face presentation taking his eyes off his prospect to glance at a shapely secretary who walked by. In a telephone conversation, the prospect can't see you listening, but he can *hear* you listening. If you fail to respond directly to his remarks, you will signal to him that you really aren't paying attention to what he says. And if he thinks that, your chances of making a sale are greatly reduced.

LISTENING TO THE NEGATIVE RESPONSE

Often a prospect will respond negatively at first to your sales presentation. If you are a good listener, you can use that response to discover what will appeal to him. For this reason, it is important that your presentation be flexible, so that you can change directions when that is indicated. For instance, a real estate agent talking to a prospect on the telephone may say, "Fred, the schools in this neighborhood are the best in the city." At this point the prospect may comment that his children are enrolled in private schools. Because of that response, the agent will no longer emphasize the schooling, and may instead point out that a particular property includes three acres of beautiful grounds. The prospect may again respond negatively: "We're not outdoor types, and we don't want to have to be slaves to our lawn." The agent now knows something further about the prospect.

While negative responses say no to a particular selling point, they are really positive signals that let the salesperson know what the prospect's needs are. After a series of such responses, the alert salesperson will have a clear picture of the prospect's buying needs, through the process of elimination. In other words, through astute listening the salesperson can recognize the prospect's "hot" buttons. Negative responses tell a good listener what it will take to encourage a positive response.

For instance, a stockbroker might say during his presentation, "Irv, would you agree with me that a 13 percent return during this period of low interest rates is an attractive return?" The client might respond negatively: "Yes, it is, but in my tax bracket I end up giving most of it to Uncle Sam." When the stockbroker hears this reply, he immediately knows that a high yield is not the thing to emphasize in his presentation to this particular client. The client has signaled that he's interested in a tax-shelter type of investment.

Now, there are times when the broker might already know this information but would still allow the client to voice his objection. In anticipation, the broker has already chosen an investment for his client in which the dividends are a non-taxable return on capital. He is then in a position to say, "Irv, that's fine. I agree with you. The yield is great. We both recognize this fact. We also agree that since you're in a 70 percent bracket, this net return is not attractive enough for you. Is that correct?" After the client has agreed with the negative statement that has been presented to him, he begins to think: Gee, here's an interesting person. He's looking out for me. This broker agrees that this isn't the best type of investment for me.

The stockbroker then continues: "Let me mention to you, Irv, that other clients of mine in circumstances like yours were also concerned about giving up 70 percent of their dividends to taxes. That's just the reason why I'm bringing this investment to your attention. Because with this investment, the majority of the dividends are a non-taxable return on capital. So here you have an opportunity to keep the majority of that cash dividend collected during the year."

In this example, the stockbroker wisely listened to a negative response, and followed it up by focusing on a situation which demanded a positive response. This is a very good technique, and the key is to listen carefully to what the client says.

IS THIS THE RIGHT TIME?

When dealing with a prospect face to face, it is usually easy to see how busy he is and whether he is able to concentrate on the presentation at this moment. In telephone selling, you must learn to listen for clues so that you can determine whether the timing is right. It may not be the most convenient and conducive time for your presentation. Perhaps he can't talk confidentially because someone else is in his office. Maybe he is trying to finish an important report and can't give you his full attention. He may have an urgent personal problem to deal with. There are countless reasons why timing may be unfavorable, and it is up to you to make sure you give your presentation under the best circumstances.

Herbert M. Swarthout, CLU, based in Kansas City, is one of the nation's leading life insurance agents. Although legally blind, Herbert is Mutual Benefit Life's top group-life agent, having produced approximately 10 percent of that company's total group coverage now in force. He comments, "In my phone conversations, I concentrate on listening to the person on the other end and giving him every opportunity to talk as much as he is willing to. But beyond this, I try to listen *in depth* to what he says—and what he really *means*. The more I can get him to talk about himself and his family, the more information I have to be of personal and professional service to him. I listen carefully to his tone of voice as a further clue to what he is saying and how he is feeling. Sometimes this concentration tells me that it is not a good time or a good day to continue the conversation. If I sense this, I try to terminate the conversation courteously and get back to him later." As Herbert knows through many years of experience, a presentation at the wrong time can mean the loss of a transaction that otherwise would have been made.

As this example illustrates, there are times when a prospect will be receptive to a presentation and times when he will not. Obviously, it is to your advantage to seek out the right times; otherwise a sale which could have been made may be lost forever. Since telephone selling is dependent upon making a large volume of calls, it's safe to assume that you will get your share of prospects who are simply in the wrong frame of mind when you call. For one reason or another, they are obviously not in a buying mood. By listening carefully and sensing their moods, you can increase your closing ratio.

There are some obvious clues when timing is not in your favor. The prospect is obviously tense or harassed; you can sense that he's in a hurry to rush you off the phone; he's simply not concentrating on what you are saying. Sometimes straightforward comments will tell you just why the circumstances are unfavorable: "I'm leaving for a two-week vacation this afternoon." "I'm attending a funeral this morning." "Our computer broke down, and this place is a madhouse today."

In making the decision to call back, the telephone salesperson must exercise caution. It is easy to grab at any excuse to avoid giving presentations, and as a result to become progressively more and more gun-shy. Therefore, keep in mind that while things may not be perfect, at least you do have the prospect on the telephone now; and you might not get another opportunity. Only under unusual circumstances should you consent to call again.

THE LONG-WINDED TALKER

There is a very fine line between sincere listening and losing control of the interview. While it is important to be a good listener, there are some prospects who simply talk too much. They will end up controlling the presentation if you let them. Furthermore, they will usually get completely off the track, greatly decreasing your chances of closing the sale.

In dealing with a talker, you must continually evaluate the interview. If the sale is sliding downhill, it will be necessary to interrupt him—but always with tact and diplomacy. Remember, you never want to insult a prospect! Instead, you should say something like "That's a very good point you just brought up, and that's precisely why . . ." At this point you can smoothly ease into your presentation and make your request for the order.

CONCLUSION

Listening is just as important in telephone selling as talking. In fact, telephone selling depends on listening considerably more than face-to-face selling, since this is the only way you have to evaluate a prospect. Always remember that everyone appreciates a good listener. A conversation which has moments of silence is not necessarily flawed. On the contrary, deliberate pauses give the prospect an opportunity to express himself.

When the prospect does talk, be sure to listen. Many people listen to words, but it takes concentration and understanding to hear the real meaning behind the words. Avoid having any distractions in your office that might interrupt your concentration on the prospect's responses. By all means, have your secretary hold any calls while you are giving a presentation, and see to it that your office arrangement is conducive to giving your undivided attention to the person on the other end of the line.

In selling, listening is just as important as talking. You cannot understand your prospect unless you hear what he says. If you listen, you will always learn something valuable. Perhaps most important, sincere, responsive listening will help you forge the lasting relationships that turn prospects into lifelong customers and loyal friends.

14.

Women in
Telephone Selling

With an ever-increasing number of women entering the work force, it is appropriate to devote a chapter to their role in telephone selling. Of course, *every* chapter in this book applies to women as well as to men, but for women there are some special advantages as well as some difficulties encountered in the field of telephone selling.

A woman who is considering entering the work force or changing careers should note that a wide range of opportunities exists in the field of telephone sales. There are positions suitable for the novice and for the experienced salesperson. A woman can enter the field part-time to supplement her family income, or she can choose a highly sophisticated field involving thousands of dollars in transactions each day. Without question, there is an opportunity to suit every woman's needs.

WORKING AT HOME

A large number of telephone saleswomen work full-time or part-time out of their own homes. For many, the opportunity to work at home is the number one attraction of telephone selling. This army of women includes mothers of young children, disabled persons, and senior citizens; and their products range from magazines to real estate.

During the course of preparing our manuscript, we interviewed many women throughout the United States. Perhaps the most prevalent comment about the advantages of telephone selling was the flexible hours. "I can set my own work schedule" was repeated time after time. This has a special appeal to young mothers who have small children to tend. Others noted that the work provided supplemental income for the family—a significant factor in light of today's spiraling inflation.

Still others stated that telephone selling in the home was more economical than the typical office job because "I don't have to spend money on such items as a fancy wardrobe and lunches. Even those coffee breaks at the vending machines add up. And I don't have to worry about gas, parking, and all those other car expenses." The consensus was that a woman can earn more by selling on the telephone at home. Even if her gross income is less, her net earnings may be greater. In the meantime, instead of having a babysitter take care of her children (another expense), she can also be a better mother. Elderly women we talked to were not only appreciative of the income they were earning but also enjoyed the opportunity to feel productive and "meet the public."

Without question, being able to work at home was highly desirable to these women. Many women said that they could not work if they had to work outside the home. And while there are numerous cottage industries, telephone selling seems to offer the most opportunity for the largest number of women.

Telephone selling at home is inherently flexible, as illustrated by one woman who sells magazine advertising to small businesses. Her favorite prospects are contractors. "Small contractors are out in the field during normal working hours," she explains. "Because I work at home, I can call them early in the morning, while my husband gets the kids ready for school, or in the evening after the family has supper. This works out so well for me, because I can schedule my household duties for those hours that aren't productive selling hours. And I generally get very good reception, because the contractors are impressed with the fact that I'm willing to call them at the times that are convenient for them."

While most women who sell by phone out of their homes do so on a part-time basis, there are many who conduct lucrative full-time businesses from their residences. For those able to make a full-time commitment, earnings can be very high. An excellent example of a very successful woman who operates a sizable business out of her home while depending heavily on the telephone is Shaindy Fenton of Fort Worth, Texas. Undoubtedly one of America's top telephone salespersons, Shaindy sells a product most people wouldn't imagine could be sold by phone: fine art, including prints, paintings, and sculptures. Ninety percent of the paintings she sells are sold by telephone, and in a good year she'll sell an estimated $10 million worth of art. She has sold some paintings worth more than $300,000 apiece—*on the telephone.* It's estimated that only a handful of art galleries in the country generate a higher annual volume than Shaindy's home-based art business.

Shaindy started her business about ten years ago, at a time when she was enthusiastically collecting prints. Since her husband was just beginning his medical practice, she wanted to supplement the family income. During a trip to New York, she visited a large print wholesaler, and he told her she could be his representative in the Dallas–Fort Worth area. "Well," Shaindy says with a laugh, "I got a suitcase full of prints and started calling on galleries and decorators. When working with the decorators, I received 10 percent of the wholesale price. After spending three hours with one particular decorator, I ended up selling him $25 worth of prints, which meant I made $2.50 on the sale. I didn't have to be a financial genius to see that I had a thankless job."

Shaindy decided to call on individuals who would be interested in starting or increasing their art collections. Her first prospects were people she and her husband had met during his military service and his internship and residency. She also placed ads in the free medical advertising journals. When people wrote in response to the ads, she followed up with telephone calls. Before long, she was getting referrals.

On her first call to a prospect, Shaindy qualifies the individual, inquiring about the kind of art he has in mind. Many of her accounts prefer investment quality art, such as the works of Jasper Johns, Rauschenberg, Miró, Picasso, or Chagall. She then sends photographs, slides, and a dossier on whatever artist the prospect is especially interested in. After the package is received, she follows up with a telephone call. "I talk about the various works available," she explains, "the artist's prices in the past and what they are now, and what I think they will be in the future. If the prospect is interested, I send him the actual art. He can send it back if he doesn't want to purchase it, but I rarely have people send back the art that I mail."

Over the years, Shaindy has built up a substantial clientele. She estimates that about 90 percent of her sales represent repeat business. About half of her new business comes from referrals. Obviously she knows how to build lasting relationships with people over the telephone. She believes the secret is to be straightforward and honest with clients. "I tell people the truth about art," she declares. "If somebody calls me and wants to buy junk art, I don't get it for him, although I could. Because I don't want to ever have to resell it. And I become 'phone friends' with my clients. I talk to them about their families and their personal lives. I build a relationship. When I'm traveling, I try to meet people I do business with who live in the area; I've probably met about half of my accounts in person. Some of my clients buy art as often as once a month. I often say, 'I don't sell art; I build collections.' This is an ongoing business, and I deal with the same people for many, many years."

In addition to making an average of thirty phone calls a day, Shaindy spends three or four hours each evening studying art. "I read about it, I think about it, I do everything around art," she bubbles. "Because I love it! The business is just perfect for me, because I also love to talk on the telephone. I've attained my girlhood dream. I talk on the phone all day—and no one tells me to get off! Once someone asked my son what I do for a living, and he said, 'My mother just lays around in bed all day and talks on the phone.'"

Shaindy makes her business sound so easy, but she didn't become one of America's top art dealers without a lot of hard work. She is organized and very conscientious. Her diligent study of art books and journals has led to her recognition as a leading authority in the field. Like other successful businesspersons, she has paid the price of success by fully preparing herself and learning her business. As a result, she has built a flourishing full-time art business in the privacy of her own home.

Women who sell from their own homes find their income is limited only by the amount of time and effort they are willing and able to put into it. In most cases, these women do not want to work full-time. In fact, the prime reason they chose telephone selling was that they wanted to pick their own hours and be free to spend time with their families during part of the day.

Joanne Katz, a communications sales consultant in Columbus, Ohio, has trained many women for companies throughout the United States. She stresses the freedom in telephone sales. "I tell them they can make anywhere from twenty-five to two hundred dollars an hour, depending on how aggressive they are. Then I add that in order to be a mother and keep that child in line, a woman has to have these aggressive qualities, whether she realizes it or not. So it's something any woman can do, if she makes up her mind to."

Joanne also assures trainees that they can plan their calling schedule around their daily routine. "It doesn't matter whether their children are infants or teenagers," she says, "there are so many people out there to call. Some of them can be called the very first thing in the morning, and some can be called late in the evening. Whenever you're free, there are prospects somewhere." Joanne stresses that women who sell from their homes must be their own bosses. "That means being organized!" she says. "You've got to have your list of prospects and their phone numbers in front of you. To quote an old cliché, you have to 'plan your work and work your plan.' "

She also points out that being your own boss and working in your own home means that discipline is vital. "There are so many distractions in the environment of your home," she admits, "that it requires a great amount of self-discipline to make those calls. This is especially true because of the amount of rejection that comes with this type of work. But I encourage women to calculate the commissions they can earn. When an aggressive woman does that, and she sees the financial possibilities, she's willing to put in the effort!"

STARTING YOUR OWN BUSINESS

Many women who have raised families and now want to re-enter the business world have developed special interests. For those who have, and who are willing to take the leap and start their own telephone business, the possibilities are endless. Shaindy Fenton is a good example of a wife and mother who combined her personal interest and expertise with a conscientious dedication to the job. As her story demonstrates, anything can be sold on the telephone. You might, for example, sell household products; maid and janitorial services; flowers and floral arrangements; real estate; advertising; employment services; lawn care; books; magazines; health products; and many, many more. You might make an arrangement with a sales organization to prospect and obtain leads. If you are skilled in fund-raising through community activities, you can do fund-raising for local organizations from your home phone for a percentage. You can arrange with a civic group to sell tickets to cultural events by phone. Whatever business occurs to you, don't shy away from selling the product because you never heard of anyone selling it by telephone. If one point has been stressed in this book above all others, it is that *anything can be sold by phone.*

There are literally hundreds of ways a creative woman can earn money selling by telephone in her home. Joanne Katz, the Columbus communications sales consultant, began her telephone selling career in advertising. With two small children at home, she decided to sell for a local magazine, *The Ohio Police.* Eventually this work developed the skills and confidence she needed to start her consulting service.

"I learned a tremendous amount about how to give a telephone sales presentation through this experience," she recalls. "The entire sales transaction was conducted by phone, and I tried to keep the conversation under five minutes. My initial approach was, 'Hi, this is Joanne Katz with *The Ohio Police.* ' Then I'd pause and give a little laugh and add, 'Nothing official.' I'd wait a few seconds and say, 'As you know, once a year we contact business and professional people for the sole purpose of raising money for our law-enforcement journal.' That 'As you know' is very effective; it makes the prospect feel he should know what you are talking about, he should be familiar with the organization. Then too, the words 'law enforcement' have a chilling effect on people. They begin to think, The police might not protect my place if I don't buy this ad.

Joanne did well selling for the magazine and then decided to start her own business in the field of publishing and advertising. "I began to check around to find out what the actual costs were," she explains, "and I learned that often as little as 18 percent of the price of the ad was going into production. The rest went for promotion costs. But I was only being paid 25 percent commission. So, after some serious soul-searching, I decided to go ahead with an idea I had. I approached a local county fair board and asked whether they had a program of events so the people coming in at the gate each day would know what was going on at the fair. They told me they didn't, because they thought it would be too expensive.

"Well, I told them I would do the program for nothing if they would simply give me the okay. They did, and I went home and started selling advertisements on the telephone—which was something I knew how to do by now. Might I mention that you *really* have enthusiasm when it's your own concept. It took me a total of six weeks to sell all the ads and put together an eight-page brochure including the ads and listing the daily events at the fair. And I made as much money on it as I had made in a full year selling for somebody else. It was terrific! And it was a real service. The people who came to the fairgrounds loved it. The program told them what was going on at any time and where to find it.

"The first two years I did the program, I contracted the artwork out, and that took 25 percent of my profits. The third year I decided to do the artwork myself, so I only had a printing cost, and everything else was profit. It was very well received. After the first year I had advertisers calling me to ask to be in it. Several abortion clinics, for instance, wanted to advertise their services, because they knew the program was reaching the youth market."

Any woman could do what Joanne did. She stresses that there are many other organizations and events that can be approached in addition to county fairs: schools, theater groups, Little Leagues, booster clubs, and so on. "Most schools, for example, lose money on their football and basketball programs," she says. "There are many sponsors, such as national beverage manufacturers or local auto dealers, who would be very interested in buying ads in those programs. So, instead of the athletic department taking a loss on the program, you can sell them on the idea that you'll do it at no cost to them. You do a service for them, and you'll end up making a good profit for yourself."

PSYCHING YOURSELF UP

Many women who sell on the telephone at home say that they sometimes find it difficult to get down to making their calls. The reason is a common problem among salespersons of every kind: the possibility of rejection. Because of the high volume of presentations a telephone salesperson makes, he or she also receives a large number of noes—almost always more noes than yeses. (Ironically, there is a direct correlation between rejections and commissions; the sales fields where the most rejections occur generally offer the highest earnings potential.) Maintaining a positive attitude in the face of rejection is absolutely vital.

If you have trouble handling rejection, you may find you put off making your calls. One woman remarks, "Once I actually sit down and get started, I can make calls for several hours—and I make good money. But there are days when I just can't force myself to get at it. I find myself doing all kinds of trivial chores around the house, anything at all to keep me from making calls." Women who have this problem often find they are emotionally exhausted after an hour or two of phone calls. It seems that, in spite of the high potential earnings, many women become gun-shy because of the high percentage of noes they receive on the telephone.

A successful Eastern stockbroker comments that she rarely calls prospects in her home town. They hang up on me too many times," she confesses. "I like to talk to people I feel comfortable with. People in the Midwest seem to be the most courteous. So I make most of my calls to Ohio, Indiana, Illinois, Iowa, and Michigan, and that's where I've developed most of my accounts."

This stockbroker finds it is very important to psyche herself up, and she does it by thinking about her clients. "They're self-made entrepreneurs," she says, "or people with responsible positions in large corporations. They're special, and I like to believe that I'm someone special too. It's very important for me to have a winning self-image. I work hard at my profession, and I hope my clients feel lucky to have me as their broker. So when somebody does act nasty on the telephone, I just say, 'Well sir, I'm terribly sorry to have disturbed you today. I thank you very much for your time, and I can assure you that I'll never call again.' Then I just hang up and forget about it. I remind myself that the vast majority of my clients have developed from cold calls, and I start thinking about all the wonderful accounts I've acquired that way—particularly my very special ones. Soon I'm thinking very positively. I *know* there's going to be somebody out there who's very special, and if I keep on calling, I'll find him. I absolutely refuse to let rejection slow me down."

Nobody, male or female, likes rejection. But as we talked to hundreds of telephone salespersons across the country, we observed that women take rejection harder than men. While men often cite a lack of self-discipline as their biggest problem in telephone selling, women frequently say that rejection depresses them and makes it hard for them to get to their calls. We won't attempt to explain *why* this is so, but it should be noted as a tendency a telephone saleswoman needs to beware of.

ADVANTAGES AND DISADVANTAGES FOR WOMEN

In telephone selling, women encounter some special obstacles; but at the same time, being a woman is often a distinct advantage. In general, once an account is established and you have had a chance to demonstrate your professionalism, clients will think of you simply as a good salesperson. Your performance becomes their only real concern. It is in the initial encounter that you are most likely to notice the advantages and disadvantages of being a woman. One stockbroker feels she encounters more initial resistance from the secretary who screens the calls than a man would. Sometimes a secretary finds it difficult to accept another woman as part of the business world. "The secretary assumes I'm placing the call for someone else. When I ask for her boss, she replies, 'Fine, I'll get him. And who are you calling for?' "

This stockbroker is very firm in saying that hostility is not the answer in situations like this. While all good telephone salespersons will make a point of being friendly to the secretary, this saleswoman believes a woman must sometimes make a special point of it. "I try to get her name as soon as possible," she says, "and I make small talk, such as 'Betty Jane, I'm calling from New York City. I've never been to Minneapolis. How's the weather out there?' Or I might ask, 'Have you ever been here?' 'Oh, yes, I visited New York about ten years ago.' This breaks the ice and lets her know that I'm on her side. She wants to help me get to talk to Mr. Brown."

A real estate agent confirms that she too finds it important to be careful in the approach to the secretary. "Who knows? She might be his wife, his daughter, or his girlfriend. So if she really insists on knowing why I'm calling, I give her all the facts, and then I appeal to her as another woman: 'Perhaps *you* can help me, Mary Ann.' Pretty soon I have her on my side. She'll say, 'You know what? I'll put that on his agenda for first thing in the morning, and I'll remind him that you'll be calling.' On the other hand, if she lets me know that I'm wasting my time, that's valuable too. I'll stop calling. Because I can make five prospecting calls in the time it takes me to put my efforts into a losing cause. I think you have to realize that a clear-cut rejection is just a time-saver for you."

A life insurance agent believes that many secretaries are suspicious of a woman calling the boss. "I think they sometimes resent being told what to do by a young female voice, and that is a barrier women have to overcome. I do it by being friendly, but very firm. I rarely leave a number. Instead I say, 'Would you please tell Mr. Smith that I'll call back. I'm so busy here, I'll be running in and out of meetings all day. Would there be a better time for me to call him back?' I always try to avoid leaving my number, because then if he *doesn't* return the call you're in a worse position. Even when I call back again and again, I say, 'No, that's all right. I'll call back again.' I won't leave my number. What I will do is I will persevere."

When they finally do speak to the prospect, some women find a little flattery helps put him in a receptive mood. "I'm so glad I finally got you on the phone, Mr. Smith. You are so busy!" In doing this, a woman salesperson is using her femininity to her advantage. But every professional we talked to agreed that there is a definite difference between that and being "sexy." Being suggestive or flirtatious is simply out of the question for a saleswoman. "If you put on a sexy act," one woman summarized, "you won't accomplish a thing businesswise. You might be propositioned, but you won't get an order. You just won't be taken seriously. Sex and business don't mix."

A telephone saleswoman can be charming without being suggestive. For instance, one young life insurance agent told about her attempt to sell a substantial group policy to a client who had purchased several policies through her. "After I had made numerous attempts to close a large group sale with him during our telephone conversation, he finally said, 'Do you know what your problem is, young lady? Nobody's ever said no to you.' I said, 'Oh no, are you going to be the first one? Are you going to disappoint me?' Well, he just loved it. How could he disappoint me? He bought the plan." This is an example of a winning, feminine response that gives a woman a distinct advantage, one that no man could get away with.

Womanliness however, should not be used deceptively. A beginning saleswoman who gets frustrated by her difficulty in reaching prospects may be tempted to pretend she is a friend in order to get through the screening. One woman in the consulting field commented on that. "I know some women who will make a cold call and say to the secretary, 'Is Bill there? Tell him Sharon is on the phone.' Well, the secretary doesn't want to ask any questions, because she figures Sharon is a girlfriend, or it's a personal call from someone he obviously knows. So the call will be put through, but it seldom accomplishes anything. If Bill doesn't blow his stack, he's at least going to be very suspicious because of the approach that was used. Even if the presentation interests him, he's going to have doubts about placing an order. That kind of deception doesn't build lasting relationships. It just isn't professional."

Many men like to get on a first-name basis with a prospect as soon as possible, and some telephone saleswomen we talked to feel the same way. The majority, however, prefer to maintain a certain professional distance. They emphasize that they never call a man by his first name unless he asks them to. "I just don't get on the phone and say, 'Hello, David, how are you?' " one woman explains. "I want to keep that distance and act professional at all times."

Another top saleswoman agrees. "I always keep it 'Mister Smith' until he lets me know he wants to change that, by saying something like 'Please, call me David.' Frankly, I think it's presumptuous to assume you have his permission to call him by his first name." These women also comment that a woman is not always taken as seriously as a man in professional sales fields, so they believe that maintaining a businesslike distance is especially important.

It certainly should never be thought that being a woman is a disadvantage in sales. On the contrary, femininity is an advantage that will make up for the social prejudices that do still exist. All telephone saleswomen, particularly those who deal in big-ticket items, run into prospects who are fascinated to find a woman in that field. Often men will say, "Tell me, miss, how did you get into the business?" A question like this is a good opening for you to talk about yourself and your company and how proud and pleased you are to be associated with them. One thoughtful saleswoman comments that many men are very interested to be called by a woman who works in "a man's field." "For the most part," she says, "they think of women in three capacities: as mothers, wives, and daughters; that's the only way they've known women. So it really intrigues them when a woman is a broker or sells sophisticated machinery. I think, overall, it's a great advantage."

All over the country, successful women who sell on the telephone believe that a woman should never pick up the phone without reminding herself that she's proud to be a woman. It's not to a saleswoman's advantage to assume a brisk, masculine attitude that doesn't reflect her personality. One West Coast investment banker comments, "I act excited, and I get emotional. And I guess some men, when I'm really bubbling about a particular investment, probably think, There she goes—a typical woman! So what? I am a woman. And it's an asset. Because I'm extraordinarily sensitive, and I care about my clients in a special way. And I believe this makes me a very special person to them. They know that I cherish my relationship with them, and that gives them confidence that I will always do my very best for them. I'm lucky to be a woman. I can show my feelings more freely than a man—and it helps create a warm, caring relationship."

CONCLUSION

The opportunities for women to sell on the telephone are tremendous, really unlimited. Positions are available to just about every woman, and in many cases it is possible to work part-time and choose your own hours. As in all commissioned sales positions, the earnings will vary greatly. Some women only want to supplement their family incomes or to keep busy a few hours a day. For others, who want to dedicate themselves full-time to their careers, six-figure incomes are within reach.

Successful telephone saleswomen express great satisfaction with the independence their achievements give them. They also enjoy the relationships they have developed with their clients over the years. Most important, they enjoy their work. To them, each call represents a challenge and each presentation is an adventure. Many stress that they could never do a kind of work that lacked the excitement of telephone selling. Above all, telephone selling is a field which permits women to be charming and womanly and at the same time become established, respected professional people.

Afterword

The telephone is the communication achievement of the twentieth century. While it has been available for quite some time, it took the energy crisis and spiraling travel costs to make the sales world take full notice of the telephone's value. With only the pressing of a few buttons, the world is at your fingertips. In seconds you're in Houston, Miami, London, or Rome. You can literally reach almost anyone, almost anywhere, in a matter of moments. Nobody can deny the time and energy the telephone saves; but in order to get results with telephone sales, you've got to master the proper techniques.

Everything you have read in this book is based on experience, not theory. Each example presents a field-tested technique that has been used by the nation's top telephone salespersons. So don't hesitate to try these techniques out. They work!

It should be emphasized once again that regardless of what you sell, with some careful thought and a bit of imagination, you can adapt many of these techniques to your product or service. In fact, trading ideas with salespersons in other fields is essential for improving your selling skills. This is an excellent way to become exposed to effective techniques which are not used in your industry. And often there's an advantage in being different from the run-of-the-mill salespersons in your field. So it is both possible and advantageous for an office machine salesperson, for example, to adopt some of the selling techniques of a successful stockbroker, or for a real estate agent to learn from a top insurance agent. In fact, there is something you can learn from salespersons in every field.

It's important to recognize the necessity of rehearsing a new selling technique prior to actually using it with a prospect. It's simply unrealistic to think that reading about the techniques described in this book will automatically make you a superstar. While you may be able to incorporate some techniques immediately, others require skill and will develop only with practice. So be prepared to spend some time rehearsing, and don't become impatient if you don't get immediate results. Role-playing and taping yourself are highly regarded methods of increasing your selling skills. When you are letter-perfect, use the new techniques, and give them time to work. Through sheer repetition during actual presentations, you will improve and begin to see a corresponding improvement in your sales productivity.

But don't expect miracles; no one becomes a great salesperson overnight. And, above all, if you don't get instant results, don't think that telephone selling doesn't work. Don't put the blame on the telephone. *It's you that's not working.* Telephone selling works for every dedicated salesperson. Remember, the suggestions in this book are based on the proven field-tested techniques of successful telephone salespersons. They *will* work for you—if you apply them properly.

While we have stated that the degree to which the telephone can be used to sell will vary from industry to industry, don't be too quick to conclude that you are in a field where one of the techniques given here does not apply. You'll be surprised at what can be done over the telephone, and at a considerably lower cost in time and money than by a sales visit. We're not implying that telephone selling will ever replace the need for face-to-face sales presentations in some industries. But the telephone can greatly increase *every* salesperson's effectiveness. And the proper use of the telephone will free up time for more face-to-face presentations, and help build loyalty in your existing clientele.

So, have a great career in selling. Your success is as close as your nearest telephone.

Index

advertising sales, 89
appointments, making of, 8–9, 35
Ary, Dick, 99
assuming-the-sale technique, 73–74
attitude:
  knowledge vs., 111
  positive, 60, 110, 111, 113–114, 115–119, 120
  see also self-image
automobile sales, 85, 89

bad news, follow-up and, 88–90, 94
Bloch, Diana, 92
Bresnan, Bill, 104–106, 107–108
Bulwer-Lytton, Edward, 110
Burnett, Bob, 93
business letters, cost of, 1
buying signals, detection of, 137

"Call Avoidance," 101
calling back, 27–29, 106, 107
  air of authority in, 28
  businesslike firmness in, 28
  and not leaving number, 158
  persistence in, 28
  timing in, 145–146
  using secretary's name in, 27–28
Carter, Shelby, Jr., 4, 9, 10, 101
clients, *see* customers
closings, 71–80

assuming-the-sale technique, 73–74
  combination of techniques in, 74
  compromise, 69, 70, 77–79
  getting agreement, 74
  major/minor, 72–73, 74
  objections as opportunity for, 60, 63, 64–65, 70
  repetition of, 65, 70, 76–77, 80
  self-confidence in, 118–119
  telephone vs. face-to-face, 71, 74, 79, 80
  urgency used in, 74–76
  wrap-up in, 79
complaints, customer, 106–108
  sympathy in handling of, 106–107
  verification of, 107
completions, 20–30
  calling back in, 27–29
  defined, 12
  finding decision-maker in, 20–22
  goals for, 12–13
  leaving message in, 26–27
  number of calls vs., 11–12
  screeners and, 22–24
  speaking with authority in, 24–26
compromise close, 69, 70, 77–79
concept, selling of, 46, 48
conference calls, 22
"conscious competence," 52
"conscious incompetence," 52

urgency *(cont.)*
  in closings, 74–76
  in handling of objections, 59–60,
    66–67

value, importance of emphasis on,
  67–68

"warm-up session," 37, 42
WATS (Wide Area Telephone
    Service) lines, 16, 102–104, 108
Wayne, John, 134
Weiler, Alan, 98–99
"windshield time," 4, 11
women, 148–161

advantages and disadvantages for,
  156–160
businesses started by, 153–155
femininity used by, 158–159
on first-name basis with prospect,
  159
in "man's field," 159–160
opportunities for, 160
rejection as problem for, 155–156
secretaries' attitudes toward, 157
sexy act and, 158
working at home by, 148–153

Xerox Corporation, 4, 10, 123
  customer service at, 101

ABOUT THE AUTHORS

The Shafiroff-Shook writing team is perhaps the most qualified in America to produce a book on telephone selling. Both men have had extensive selling careers, and Bob Shook has had nine other books published. They have combined their talent and experience to create the most comprehensive guide to telephone selling ever written.

Martin Shafiroff is one of America's leading investment salespersons. He has generated security transactions in the hundreds of millions of dollars. A good deal of his time is spent reviewing the various research proposals presented by his firm.

His main responsibility today is working with individuals throughout the country advising and recommending investments in securities, real estate, and tax shelters. It is believed that he deals with more board chairmen and presidents of corporations than any other investment broker in America.

He began his career in investments in 1966, and has been associated with a major investment banking firm since then.

Martin has given numerous lectures on the art of investing and the psychology of telephone communications. He has been the subject of feature articles in *The Wall Street Journal*, *The Institutional Investor*, and the Harper & Row book *Ten Greatest Salespersons*.

Perhaps no business is more telephone-oriented than the securities industry. Marty's success shows what can be done *on the telephone* by any salesperson who is dedicated to using the most effective techniques. While Marty is now well known, and the name of Lehman Brothers opens doors, he did not inherit his success. Instead, like Bob Shook, he earned it—on the telephone. Both men believe that every dedicated salesperson has the same opportunity to achieve.

Bob Shook graduated from Ohio State University in 1959, having majored in insurance. He spent two years as a representative for a clothing manufacturer, and then he and his father, Herb, opened an insurance agency in the basement of the Shook home. The father-son business, originally capitalized with $1,000, grew into one of the nation's largest privately owned insurance agencies. Shook Associates Corporation operated in twenty-four states with several hundred full-time agents.

During his years as an agent in the field, Bob became interested in developing techniques for prospecting and qualifying over the telephone, even though insurance has long been considered a face-to-face selling industry. Many of the follow-up techniques given in *Successful Telephone Selling in the 80s* are also a result of Bob's work with telephone follow-up in the insurance industry.

The latter part of Bob's insurance career was devoted to sales management, where he pioneered the use of the telephone in prospecting for, qualifying, and recruiting new agents, an ongoing concern in an industry which traditionally has a high turnover.

In 1974, the Shooks founded American Executive Life Insurance Company. Five years later, having written four books while serving as the company's first chairman of the board, Bob decided to write full-time. To date, most of his books have been business-oriented *(The Entrepreneurs, Winning Images* and *The Chief Executive Officers)* and sales-oriented *(The Complete Professional Salesman, The Real Estate People, Ten Greatest Salespersons).*